JAY YANG

You Can Just Do Things

The Power of Permissionless Action

First published by Jay Yang, LLC 2025

Copyright © 2025 by Jay Yang

All rights reserved. No part of this publication may be reproduced, stored or transmitted in any form or by any means, electronic, mechanical, photocopying, recording, scanning, or otherwise without written permission from the publisher. It is illegal to copy this book, post it to a website, or distribute it by any other means without permission.

This book is written as a source of information only. The information contained in this book should by no means be considered a substitute for the advice, decisions, or judgment of the reader's professional or financial advisors. All efforts have been made to ensure the accuracy of the information contained in this book as of the date published. The author expressly disclaims responsibility for any adverse effects arising from the use or application of the information contained herein.

First edition

ISBN (paperback): 979-8-9924592-0-3
ISBN (hardcover): 979-8-9924592-1-0
ISBN (digital): 979-8-9924592-2-7

Cover art by Jean Aubrey Cayabyab

This book was professionally typeset on Reedsy. Find out more at reedsy.com

To Max, for keeping my feet on the ground while my head is up in the clouds.

"Life can be much broader, once you discover one simple fact, and that is, everything around you that you call life was made up by people that were no smarter than you. And you can change it, you can influence it, you can build your own things that other people can use."

– Steve Jobs

Contents

Foreword   iii
Prologue   1
Introduction   6

I   PART I: PREPARATION

 1   DON'T BURN THE BOATS   13
 2   DEFINE YOUR NORTH STAR   17
 3   BE A LEARNING MACHINE   22
 4   REVERSE ENGINEER THE GREATS   26
 5   THERE'S NO SPEED LIMIT   32
 6   EMBRACE OBSESSION   37
 7   BE A SUPER CONNECTOR   42
 8   LEARN TO SELL   48
 9   DO THE WORK UPFRONT   52

II   PART II: CREATION

10   STRIKE WHILE THE IRON IS HOT   59
11   GO WHERE THE ACTION IS   65
12   MAKE YOUR MOVE   71
13   A SHAMELESS ASK   80
14   CREATE YOUR OWN ROLE   82
15   DIVE THROUGH CRACKED DOORS   89

16	GIVE THE EXTRA OUNCE	94
17	WORK IN PUBLIC	100
18	GET IN THE ARENA	107
19	STAY IN THE GAME	112
20	TRY THE HANDLE	117

PERMISSIONLESS REFLECTION	122
ACKNOWLEDGMENTS	124
FURTHER READING	127
SELECTED BIBLIOGRAPHY	128
About the Author	132

Foreword

I wasn't looking to hire anyone when Jay Yang first reached out. I get hundreds of pitches a week—most of them generic, uninspired, or downright lazy. But this one? This one stopped me in my tracks.

Jay was 17 years old. A senior in high school living with his parents. That's not usually the profile of someone I'd hire to help run my marketing. But then I opened his email. Inside was a 19-slide deck that dissected everything wrong with my social media and email marketing. He didn't just point out the flaws—he proposed solutions. And then, to make sure I had no reason to say no, he included nine ready-to-publish pieces of content.

He didn't ask for permission. He didn't say, "Can I help?" or, "What do you need from me?" He just did the work. No fluff, no fanfare. He showed me exactly how he could make my life easier.

And guess what? He got the job.

That's the essence of what you're about to read in *You Can Just Do Things*.

Jay's story reminds me of my own journey. Back in 2006, I was blown away by a product called Mint.com. I wanted to work with them so badly that I pitched myself for the Director of Marketing role. The founder, Aaron Patzer, laughed me off. "You don't know anything about marketing," he said. Ouch. But he wasn't wrong.

But instead of walking away, I went home, read every marketing book I could find, and spent 80 hours building a detailed launch plan—for free. Then I emailed it to Aaron and said, "If you like this, let me run it for three months. If it works, you can pay me." He said yes, we executed the plan, and Mint sold for $170 million three years later.

Jay's pitch hit me the same way. He wasn't some industry veteran with a decade of expertise. He didn't have a stacked resume or big credentials. What he had was effort. He put in the work before anyone asked him to. He showed me what he could do, made my life easier, and left me no choice but to say yes.

This isn't just about landing a job. The lessons in this book apply to every corner of your life. Want to start a business? Instead of asking for funding, build something that works to validate the idea. Want to grow your network? Don't ask people how you can help them—figure it out and show them. Want to change your career? Start doing the work before anyone pays you to do it.

Jay has done a phenomenal job weaving together these stories and strategies into a clear, actionable roadmap. Whether you're trying to land your dream job, pitch a client, or take your first step as an entrepreneur, this book gives you the tools to make it impossible for the world to ignore you.

If you take away one thing from this foreword, let it be this: don't wait. Don't wait for permission. Don't wait for someone to notice you. Don't wait for the "right time." Start now. Start messy. Start where you are. The tools are out there. The opportunities are out there. But it's up to you to take the first step.

– Noah Kagan
Author of *Million Dollar Weekend*

Prologue

THE CURSOR BLINKED at the bottom of my email.

I had rewritten it at least a dozen times, tweaking every word. It had to be sharp but not desperate. Confident but not arrogant.

The subject line read: **Big Fan of beehiiv.**

Inside was a detailed pitch deck for a course idea I had put together—one that I believed could help beehiiv's users get more out of the platform. There was no job posting. No open internship position. Just me, a 16-year-old high school kid, taking a shot at working with my favorite company.

I stared at the screen, my finger hovering over the send button.

What if he ignored it? Worse—what if he thought I was a joke?

I had no credentials. Little experience. And frankly, no reason to be taken seriously. But I knew one thing: waiting never gets you anywhere.

I took a breath. *Screw it.* I hit send.

The next morning, I woke up and checked my inbox... One

new email.

Tyler Denk – Re: Big Fan of beehiiv.

My chest tightened as I clicked.

He liked my idea! He wanted to hop on a call.

Two weeks later, I was working directly with Tyler, beehiiv's co-founder and CEO, and the marketing team. I had landed an internship at a high-growth startup.

I was inside the walls. And I had gotten there without a degree, without a résumé, without anyone's permission. That one email—one shot in the dark—completely changed how I saw the world.

It made me realize how many opportunities are just sitting there, waiting to be taken. How often do we hold back—not because we aren't capable, but because we assume we aren't ready?

For a long time, I thought success meant checking all the right boxes. I was a straight-A student, varsity basketball player, and "model kid." I worked hard, did what I was supposed to do, and stayed on the well-marked path. But the older I got, the more I felt boxed in. The rules were good for keeping me safe, but they left little room for me to think or create on my own.

Then I stumbled upon "Money Twitter", an online community of people building businesses, sharing self-improvement ideas, and striving to live life on their own terms. They weren't waiting for someone to hand them an opportunity; they were making their own. It was electrifying. And I wanted to be like them.

The problem? I had no idea how. I tried a music promotion YouTube channel. I started a clothing brand. I ran several Instagram theme pages. None of them made me rich. None of them went viral. None of them unlocked some secret formula for success. Instead, I spent months creating content that barely reached anyone and chasing ideas that never took off. It felt pointless, like I was spinning my wheels and getting nowhere.

But looking back, none of it was wasted. Each of those failures was a step forward. They weren't dead ends. They were experiments. They taught me how to spot opportunities, test ideas, and adapt when things didn't work. Most importantly, they taught me that action—any action—is the best antidote to doubt.

A few months after landing the beehiiv internship, I used the same Permissionless approach with Noah Kagan, the founder of AppSumo. Instead of asking if he was hiring, I sent him a 19-page pitch deck outlining exactly how he could improve his email and social media funnel. I included nine ready-to-publish pieces of content. I didn't just tell him what I could do—I showed him.

Each opportunity snowballed into another. By the time I turned 18, I had built a marketing agency from scratch, worked with multimillionaire clients, and grown a social media following that reached hundreds of thousands—all while still in high school. My clients flew me across the country. I took calls between classes and spent my free periods binge-listening to business podcasts. School still mattered, but it was no longer the center of my world. I was building something bigger—on my terms.

None of this was supposed to happen.

I wasn't some natural-born entrepreneur. I wasn't the kid selling candy out of his backpack. If anything, I was a nerd. My mom used to hide books from me because I'd wake up at four in the morning to read them. Whether it was The *Magic Treehouse* or the *Alex Rider* spy series, once I started, I couldn't stop. In school, I'd race through homework and quizzes just so I could get back to reading.

I grew up in an Asian household where respect, discipline, and obedience were the foundation. My parents weren't tiger parents, but they did set clear expectations: work hard, follow the rules, and stay on the well-marked path. For years, I stuck to that script. But the truth is, most traditional paths aren't designed for speed. They promise stability but deliver stagnation. They ask you to wait your turn in a system built for slow, linear progress while the most meaningful opportunities are taken by those willing to step outside the lines.

This book isn't about being reckless. It's about understanding when and how to break the rules strategically to create opportunities. Life isn't a straight path with clear instructions. It's a maze, and those who succeed aren't the ones who wait for the main door to open. They're the ones who find a side entrance, carve their own way forward, or knock the whole wall down.

The truth is, you don't need experience to start. You don't need connections to contribute. What you need is the willingness to act without waiting for permission.

I didn't write this book because I've mastered this mindset (I'm still learning). I wrote it because it's the book I wish I had when I was starting out, trying to navigate a world where traditional paths didn't seem to fit.

If this book does anything, I hope it leaves you with fewer excuses and more questions:

What are you waiting for?
Who are you waiting on?
And why not you?

Because the only permission that matters is the one you give yourself.

Introduction

We're taught that you need a publisher to write a book, a studio to make a movie, or a gatekeeper to deem you worthy. But the truth is, the tools to create and share have never been more accessible. The only permission you need is your own.
—Austin Kleon (Author of *Steal Like An Artist*)

MAYBE YOU'RE JUST starting out—fresh out of school, staring down a world that feels impossible to break into. Maybe you've been at this for years, climbing a path that no longer feels like your own. Maybe you're circling a big idea, waiting for the perfect moment to begin, unsure if you're ready.

Wherever you are, the biggest obstacle isn't what you think it is. It's not your résumé, your network, or your bank account. It's waiting. Waiting for permission. Waiting to be chosen. Waiting for someone else to say, "It's your turn."

We're taught to wait our entire lives. The story goes like this: work hard, follow the rules, wait your turn, and eventually, someday, you'll be rewarded. It's a comforting narrative—one that makes the world feel fair and predictable. But what if it's not true? What if the ladder everyone is climbing leads nowhere?

INTRODUCTION

What if success isn't about waiting at all—but about creating your own opportunities?

This book is about embracing Permissionless Action in a world that trains us to seek approval. It's about realizing that the biggest breakthroughs come when you stop asking for someone else's green light and give yourself permission to start.

In this book, you'll see how Taylor Swift convinced her family to move to Nashville so she could chase her dream of becoming a country musician. How Sam Walton spent his early years borrowing ideas from competitors to build Walmart into a retail empire. And how James Dyson, frustrated by the inefficiency of vacuum cleaners, built his own that revolutionized the industry.

You'll discover how Kobe Bryant became one of basketball's greatest not just through talent, but by obsessively breaking down film, stealing moves from past legends, and rebuilding his game piece by piece. How Jeff Bezos walked away from a lucrative Wall Street job to launch an idea no one else believed in. And how Sidney Weinberg, a high school dropout, turned a janitor's assistant job at Goldman Sachs into a CEO position.

Could these individuals have achieved what they did by waiting for permission? By sticking to the prescribed path or waiting until they felt ready? Of course not. Their success wasn't about talent, luck, or resources—it was about their willingness to act, even in the face of uncertainty.

You might think, "But I'm not like them. I don't have their

resources, their connections, or their advantages."

That's exactly what they thought too. None of them started with certainty. They started with doubt. They started with fear. They started with every reason to believe it might not work.

You might also think, "But what if I fail?"

It's a valid fear. No one wants to fall flat on their face. But here's the truth: failure isn't the opposite of success—it's part of it.

Sam Walton made countless early business mistakes, including losing his first successful store due to a bad lease, before he learned the lessons that built Walmart. James Dyson built 5,127 prototypes of his vacuum cleaner before finally nailing the model. And Kobe Bryant missed more shots than most players ever take.

What separates them isn't the absence of failure—it's their ability to keep going despite it. To learn, adapt, and act again.

The real question isn't, "What if I fail?" The real question is, "What happens if I never try?"

This is not a book about taking shortcuts or defying the rules for its own sake. It's not a book that promises overnight success or guarantees that every risk will pay off. It's also not an instruction manual filled with step-by-step hacks. There are plenty of self-help books that will teach you the tactics of success, but tactics are fleeting. As Harrington Emerson is attributed with saying, "Tactics are many, principles are few. The person who understands principles can choose their own methods."

Instead, this book is about The Permissionless Approach—a timeless, universal approach to creating opportunities in a world that often tells you to wait your turn.

To bring this principle to life, this book will contain ideas, challenges, and stories from history that illustrate the timeless power of Permissionless Action. Stories of people who refused to wait, who acted when others hesitated, and who built extraordinary lives not because they were fearless or privileged, but because they chose to take the first step.

This book is divided into two parts:

1. **Preparation:** Success starts long before the opportunity arrives. This section will teach you how to sharpen your focus, build valuable skills, and position yourself to spot—and seize—opportunities others miss. Preparation isn't glamorous, but it's the stage that separates the dreamers from the doers.
2. **Creation:** This is where you step out of the shadows and into the arena. You'll learn how to bypass gatekeepers, stand out, and make bold moves—even when you feel unready.

Each part is designed to meet you where you are. Whether you're starting from scratch or looking to reinvent yourself, you'll find tools, strategies, and inspiration to take the next step. You'll learn how to think differently, act boldly, and solve problems in ways that get noticed.

You don't have to be fearless. You don't have to be perfect. You just have to start.

This book is your permission slip. But the truth is, you've always had it.

Let's get to work.

I

PART I: PREPARATION

WHAT IS PREPARATION? Preparation is laying the groundwork for success before the opportunity arrives. It's the quiet, deliberate work that sets the stage for bold moves. While others wait for the right moment, preparation ensures you're ready when it comes—or creates the moment yourself. It's about mastering the fundamentals, building skills, and positioning yourself to seize opportunities others overlook.

1

DON'T BURN THE BOATS

The art of war teaches us to rely not on the likelihood of the enemy's not coming, but on our own readiness to receive him; not on the chance of his not attacking, but rather on the fact that we have made our position unassailable.
— Sun Tzu (Chinese Military Strategist)

IN 2004, a young Mark Zuckerberg was sitting on a goldmine. Facebook had launched, and it was rapidly gaining traction at Harvard. But Zuckerberg didn't drop out of college the day he hit "publish" on the site. He waited. He worked. He built momentum. By the time he left Harvard, Facebook wasn't a vague idea or a long-shot gamble. It was a platform with proven traction and over 1 million users.

Hollywood likes to glorify the daredevil entrepreneur, the bold hero who leaps without looking. The truth is, most success stories aren't stories of recklessness—they're stories of preparation. Zuckerberg left Harvard when he didn't have to bet the farm. He reduced his risk, positioned himself for success, and ensured his foundation was solid before taking the leap.

Too often, we think success is about seeing the future clearly. If only we could predict the next big trend, the next market crash, or the next revolutionary technology, we'd be unstoppable. But the world doesn't work like that. You can't predict what will happen tomorrow, let alone five years from now. What you can do is position yourself to thrive no matter what happens.

Marc Randolph, the co-founder and first CEO of Netflix, explained it simply: "Don't obsess about predicting the future. Instead, put yourself in a position where you're poised to take advantage of whatever happens next."

When you're well-positioned, time becomes your ally. When you're poorly positioned, it becomes your enemy.

Take Elon Musk, for example. Before he founded Tesla and SpaceX, Elon had already sold his first startup, Zip2, and his stake in PayPal. The multiple millions he made gave him the runway to take massive risks without jeopardizing his financial stability. Musk didn't leap into the unknown with empty pockets. He built his foundation first.

In his book *Clear Thinking*, Shane Parrish compares it to playing Tetris: when you're doing well, you have options. Every piece fits somewhere. But when you're in a bad spot, you need exactly the right piece to survive. Success isn't about predicting what piece will come next—it's about creating a position where *any* piece can work.

The same principle extends across disciplines. Athletes practice plays before running them in the game. They refine, iterate, and improve until the moves are second nature. By the time they take the field, they're not experimenting—they're executing. Before writing his popular book *The Obstacle Is the Way*, Ryan Holiday validated his ideas with shorter articles and blog posts. Startups use the same approach. Before going all in on an idea, they create a minimum viable product to test whether it works. If it does, they invest more. If it doesn't, they adjust.

If you've heard the phrase "burn the boats," you might think that commitment requires eliminating every safety net. But that's not how most great successes happen. When I worked with Noah Kagan, one of the most popular concepts he talked about was not quitting his day job until he hit his "freedom number"—the amount of money you need to be earning on the side to quit your day job comfortably. It's a simple equation: identify your core needs—rent, food, dependent expenses—and calculate the minimum amount needed to cover these essentials.

Here's the good news: your position isn't fixed. Every choice you make—saving money, learning a new skill, connecting with like-minded individuals—strengthens your foundation.

The first part of this book is about those choices. About what it takes to prepare for Permissionless Action when no one is watching. Preparation isn't sexy, but it's the work that makes everything else possible.

This is how leaps of faith happen. Not with a spur-of-the-moment bold decision, but with many quiet moments of preparation that make the leap possible.

They say the tallest buildings require the deepest foundations. Well, now it's time to set your foundation.

2

DEFINE YOUR NORTH STAR

And those who were seen dancing were thought to be insane by those who could not hear the music.
— Friedrich Nietzsche (German Philosopher)

THE CLANG OF METAL WEIGHTS ECHOED through the dimly lit gym. The air smelled faintly of sweat and iron. Faded posters of bodybuilding legends clung to the walls, their edges curling with age. Arnold Schwarzenegger tightened his grip on the barbell, his muscles trembling from exhaustion.

He was the only one there that early, grinding through his grueling twice-a-day workout regimen. Mornings were for heavy compound lifts—bench presses, squats, and deadlifts—while evenings focused on isolating specific muscle groups and perfecting his form.

Outside, the small Austrian village where he grew up was quiet, a place where life moved slowly and ambitions rarely strayed beyond its borders. But Arnold was different. "Normal people can be happy with a regular life," he reflected. "I was different. I felt there was more to life than just plodding through an average existence."

On his bedroom walls were posters of Reg Park, the legendary bodybuilder-turned-movie-star. To Arnold, Park wasn't just a hero—he was the blueprint. Park's journey from gym floors to the silver screen planted a seed in Arnold's mind: if Park could do it, he could too. "The model was there in my mind," Arnold later said. "I only had to grow enough to fill it."

Arnold trained with unrelenting focus, biking eight miles to the gym and pushing his body past its limits. After one particularly intense workout, he was so sore he couldn't even hold onto his bike handles, falling off mid-ride. Numb and exhausted, he pushed the bike home, leaning on it for support.

He immersed himself not just in the physical grind but in the study of bodybuilding. Arnold dissected muscle magazines, studied anatomy, and closely observed the techniques of champions. His friends mocked his obsession, but Arnold pressed on, fueled by a vision they couldn't see. Every rep, every bead of sweat, and every ache was a step closer to the future he was determined to create.

Arnold's perseverance paid off. In 1967, at just 20 years old, he became the youngest Mr. Universe in history. That victory was the first of many. He dominated bodybuilding, winning Mr. Olympia seven times and redefining what was possible in the sport.

Arnold's story highlights a vital lesson: knowing exactly what you want creates the drive needed to achieve it.

The truth is, most people don't lack motivation; they lack clarity. Arnold knew exactly what he wanted. He wanted to become the best bodybuilder in the world. This clarity drove every decision he made. While his peers partied, he trained. While others doubted him, he doubled down on his vision. Without a clear North Star, you're adrift, chasing goals that belong to someone else or none at all. To define your North Star, ask yourself: If you could design your dream life, what would it look like?

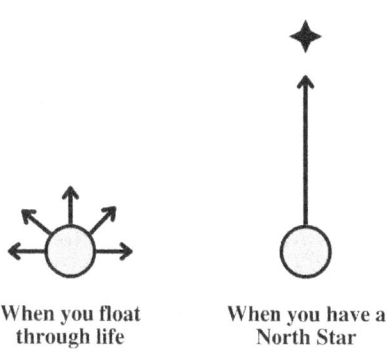

When you float through life   **When you have a North Star**

Picture your ideal day. Where are you? What are you working on? Who surrounds you? Write it down, every detail. Be as specific as possible. What kind of car do you drive? What's your energy like? How do you spend your weekends? It will be messy at first, but perfection is not the point. It's about getting your first iteration out of the way so you can refine it.

Next, define what you don't want. Reflect on the life you'd find unbearable. Is it being stuck in a nine-to-five with no room for creativity? Or perhaps it's a career that offers financial rewards but no fulfillment? Or maybe it's having a large gut and feeling sluggish all day. These anti-goals are just as important as your aspirations because they help you steer clear of paths that don't serve you.

Finally, to keep your North Star front and center, make it impossible to ignore. Set a reminder that interrupts your daily routine—a sticky note on your laptop, a phrase etched onto your journal's first page, or a single sentence as your phone's lock screen. Some of the most disciplined people in the world tattoo their goals onto their skin, not because they need decoration, but because they refuse to forget what they're aiming for.

Arnold's journey wasn't a straight line to success. He faced setbacks, ridicule, and moments of doubt–just like many others whose stories you'll read in the upcoming chapters. But he was able to overcome those obstacles because he had a clear vision of what he wanted. When your purpose is strong enough, you stop caring what others think.

Define your North Star, commit to it, and let it guide your choices. Because the only thing worse than failing is climbing a mountain, only to realize it's the wrong one.

Permissionless Challenge:

Write down, in vivid detail, what you want. Be specific, but don't worry about it being perfect. Just get it down. Then write down what you don't want—the version of life you're determined to avoid. Finally, choose where you'll place your North Star to keep your vision front and center.

3

BE A LEARNING MACHINE

An investment in knowledge pays the best interest.
— Benjamin Franklin

THE WOODEN FLOORS of the store creaked under Sam Walton's boots. He crouched near the shelves, pretending to browse. His sharp eyes scanned the layout, the product placement, the flow of customers. Every detail mattered. This wasn't his store—at least, not yet. Walton's leather notebook was open, and his pencil moved quickly as he captured ideas. It wasn't stealing, he told himself. It was learning.

Sam Walton, the founder of Walmart, wasn't always a retail icon. In the late 1940s, he was a scrappy entrepreneur running a variety store in Newport, Arkansas, barely making ends meet. His days started early and ended late, often with a long drive to competitor stores. He would study everything he could about their stores. What drew customers' eyes? Why were certain products placed near the register? How did pricing strategies differ from his own? He talked to employees, bought small items to examine receipts, and took detailed notes. "If someone else is doing it better," Walton wrote in his autobiography, "why not copy it?"

One of these trips led him to a store two towns over. It was thriving in a way his store wasn't. Walton noticed brightly colored signage directing attention, high-margin items placed at eye level, and slower-moving products near checkout lines. Back in Newport, he tested these techniques. Within weeks, sales in previously overlooked sections started climbing. His notebook had become a guide, each page filled with ideas to test.

Another pivotal moment came during a visit to St. Louis. Walton stepped into a grocery store and froze. Customers were pushing carts—self-service carts that allowed them to roam freely and gather more items. Walton immediately saw the potential. "Why hadn't we thought of this?" he muttered. The next day, he introduced self-service carts at his own store. The results were immediate and transformative.

Walton's relentless commitment to learning defined his career. He wasn't content to simply run a store; he wanted to understand every detail of retailing. In the 1970s, that same curiosity led him to invest $500 million in computer systems for Walmart—an astronomical sum at the time. While competitors hesitated, Walton saw a chance to revolutionize inventory management. Daily reports showed what sold, what didn't, and where adjustments were needed. It gave Walmart a real-time edge no other retailer could match.

"Most everything I've done," Walton reflected, "I've copied from somebody else." His genius wasn't in creating ideas from scratch but in spotting what worked, acting on it quickly, and refining it endlessly.

Walton's story is a reminder that ignorance carries a price tag. Every skill you don't learn, every opportunity you miss, every insight you overlook—these add up to a cost you pay over your lifetime. This is what serial entrepreneur and investor Alex Hormozi calls "Ignorance Debt".

Imagine someone earning $50,000 a year. They dream of making a million but don't know how. Every year they remain at $50,000, they're paying $950,000 in ignorance debt. It's daunting, sure, but also empowering. Why? Because it's fully within your control.

If you're an athlete, ignorance debt might mean not knowing the best training methods or recovery techniques that could elevate your performance. For a musician, it could mean missing out on understanding music production or building a personal brand to grow your audience. The gap between where you are and where you could be isn't just about effort—it's about knowing *where* to focus that effort.

If you want to pay it down, you have to take responsibility for your education.

Too many people let learning come to them. They wait for school to teach them or complain about how inefficient formal education is. But the truth is, nobody is responsible for your learning except you.

If you're serious about growing, you need to design your own curriculum. This next chapter will show you how.

4

REVERSE ENGINEER THE GREATS

To be ignorant of what occurred before you were born is to remain always a child. For what is the worth of human life, unless it is woven into the life of our ancestors by the records of history?
— Marcus Tullius Cicero (Roman Statesman)

KOBE BRYANT had nothing left to prove in 2008. He had already won 3 NBA championships, countless accolades, and was considered one of the best basketball players of all time. But to Kobe, the game was never about what he'd already done—it was about what he could still become.

So there he was, in a quiet corner of the Team USA practice court, long after his teammates had called it a day. He wasn't taking more shots or running plays. He was studying.

Weeks earlier, Kobe had been watching tapes of Hakeem Olajuwon, the Hall of Fame center known for his impeccable post moves. Footwork that made defenders stumble over themselves. Spins and pivots so smooth they seemed choreographed.

Hakeem's game was nothing like Kobe's. Hakeem was a center; Kobe was a guard. The post was for big men who bulldozed through opponents, not guards who glided across the floor. But that's exactly what drew Kobe to it.

Night after night, he slowed the film, rewound it, and studied every feint, every spin, every subtle shift of weight. Then, he practiced—one move, a hundred times.

The next season, the Lakers won the championship. Those post moves—moves learned from a retired big man—became some of Kobe's most dangerous weapons. But this wasn't new for Kobe. He had always been a student of the game, always looking for an edge.

It started in high school, long before he was the Black Mamba.

Most teenagers filled their nights with parties, video games, or endless phone calls. Not Kobe. After practice, while his friends unwound or went to bed, he would disappear into the small den in his family's home. The room was dimly lit, its TV screen flickering with grainy basketball footage.

This was his ritual. Hours of film study, night after night. Alone, except for the occasional presence of his high school girlfriend, Jocelyn Ebron, who sometimes sat beside him. She would recall later, "He wanted to watch them all the time."

Kobe wasn't just watching for entertainment. He was deconstructing the game. His eyes darted across the screen, studying every detail: the spacing, the angles, the footwork. Every flick of the wrist, every pivot, every movement—he filed it away.

Sometimes, the tapes were of himself. He studied his mistakes, his tendencies, and where his form broke down. Other times, they were of Michael Jordan.

He rewound the clips of Jordan's fadeaway jumper over and over again, until he could see the mechanics in his sleep. How Jordan planted his left foot, leaned back just enough to create separation, and released the ball at its apex. Kobe would write mental notes, then go to the gym and replicate it, step for step.

Years later, Bryant would openly admit: "I stole a lot of his moves."

It wasn't exciting. It wasn't flashy. It was hours in a dark room, pen and paper in hand, watching film while the rest of the world slept.

And it paid off. By the time Kobe entered the NBA, his game already bore the marks of Jordan: the same deadly fadeaway, the same killer instinct, the same mastery of footwork that made defenders hopeless. People called him the next Michael Jordan, and in some ways, he was.

But what they missed was this: Kobe didn't become great by accident. He studied greatness. He reverse-engineered it. And he made it his own.

This relentless curiosity wasn't unique to Kobe. Wayne Gretzky, widely considered the greatest hockey player of all time, approached the game the same way.

When Gretzky was fourteen, his coach pulled him aside after practice. "Go home and watch Bobby Clarke tonight," he told him. Clarke was an undersized forward for the Philadelphia Flyers—tough, smart, crafty.

Later that night, Gretzky sat front of the TV. Pen in hand, Gretzky traced the path of the puck onto a blank sheet of paper. Without looking, he followed every pass, every shot, every rebound. When Clarke went to the bench, Gretzky would pause and examine his work. What patterns emerged? Where did Clarke go that others didn't?

He noticed that Clarke played out of the corners. Instead of fighting in front of the net, he used the space behind it— unmarked territory that no one else had thought to exploit.

Gretzky adopted the habit. On the ice, he stopped trying to muscle through opponents and instead floated to where the puck would be. He turned corners and behind-the-net space into his personal playground.

Years later, Gretzky held 61 NHL records. People called him a genius, but to him, it wasn't magic. It was the result of studying the game—and the players who'd mastered it—better than anyone else.

The same principle applies to any craft. John Mayer, one of the greatest guitarists of his generation, once described how he approached learning music: "Whatever you learn is the tip of the iceberg. Dive underwater and find the rest of the iceberg."

When Mayer learned a riff or chord progression, he didn't stop there. He immersed himself in the work of blues icons like B.B. King, Stevie Ray Vaughan, and Jimi Hendrix. He studied their playing styles, their phrasing, and their emotional expression. But Mayer didn't stop there. He looked further, uncovering the influences that shaped his heroes, connecting the threads of a musical lineage that extended back decades.

This idea isn't new, but it remains timeless. In *Steal Like an Artist*, Austin Kleon advises: "Study everything there is to know about [a thinker], then find three people that thinker loved and find out everything about them. Repeat this as many times as you can. Climb up the tree as far as you can go. Once you climb your own tree, it's time to grow your own branch."

Most people think learning is a chore, a tedious process of accumulating knowledge. But the greats know the truth: learning is theft.

Someone smarter than you has spent years—sometimes decades—beating their head against the wall to solve the exact problem you're facing. Why start from scratch when you can steal that hard-won knowledge and make it yours?

That is power.

In the age of the internet, this process has never been more accessible. You can watch Ivy League lectures on YouTube, explore NASA's research archives, or read shareholder letters from your favorite companies.

What made Kobe, Gretzky, and Mayer extraordinary wasn't just their extraordinary ability—it was their willingness to study those who had come before them.

The greats left us a map. The question is, will you follow it?

> **Permissionless Challenge:**
> Find someone who's already achieved what you're chasing. Study them obsessively. Watch their interviews. Read what they've written. Break down their routines, habits, and decisions. *What did they do that you're not doing yet?*
>
> Then, take ONE action this week that moves you closer to their level.

5

THERE'S NO SPEED LIMIT

The world is a very malleable place. If you know what you want, and you go for it with maximum energy and drive and passion, the world will often reconfigure itself around you much more quickly and easily than you would think.
— Marc Andreessen (Co-creator of the first widely used web browser)

IN THE EARLY 1990s, Derek Sivers was a 17-year-old musician preparing to attend Berklee College of Music, one of the most prestigious institutions for aspiring artists. Like many incoming students, he was excited, eager—and maybe a little unsure of what was coming.

A few weeks before school began, Derek came across an ad in the paper for a local recording studio in Chicago. Curious about music typesetting, he called the number, expecting a simple answer. On the other end of the line was Kimo Williams, the studio owner and a Berklee alumnus. When Kimo heard Derek was heading to Berklee, he didn't just answer the question—he issued a challenge.

"I have a theory," Kimo said. "With the right training, I can help you graduate in two years. Come by my studio tomorrow at 9:00 AM. No charge."

For Derek, this wasn't blind luck. He was the kind of person who followed his curiosity and took action. He could have ignored the ad or hesitated to make the call, but he didn't. When the opportunity presented itself, he didn't overthink it—he showed up the next morning, early but waiting outside until exactly 8:59 before ringing the bell.

Kimo wasn't just another studio musician—he was a Berklee graduate who had built a career composing music that defied boundaries, blending jazz fusion, classical symphonies, and rock. His compositions had been performed by symphonies, celebrated by critics, and shaped by the discipline of being a Vietnam veteran. If anyone could collapse years of learning into hours, it was Kimo.

Kimo wasted no time. He sat Derek down at the piano and started explaining complex jazz harmonies: substitute chords, tri-tones, resolution theory. He didn't just lecture—he made Derek apply the concepts on the spot. Kimo crammed months of material into hours, pushing Derek to keep up. It was fast. It was overwhelming. And it was thrilling.

By the end of the first three-hour lesson, Derek had absorbed an entire semester's worth of Berklee's harmony curriculum. Over the next four lessons, Kimo covered four more semesters.

When Derek arrived at Berklee, he tested out of six semesters of classes.

Six semesters. Just gone.

While his peers spent years plodding through the basics, Derek surged ahead. But he didn't stop there. Kimo had shown him what was possible, and Derek took the lesson to heart. He began teaching himself additional classes, buying course materials, completing the work on his own, and taking final exams for credit. By challenging the traditional pace of the system, Derek graduated with a bachelor's degree in just two and a half years. He was twenty.

Years later, Derek reflected on what Kimo taught him: *"The system is designed so anyone can keep up. But if you're more driven than most people, you can do way more than anyone expects. There's no speed limit."*

Most people assume success follows a linear process—one semester at a time, one promotion at a time, one carefully measured step after another. These systems weren't designed for excellence; they were designed to accommodate the average person.

The standard pace feels safe. It gives us excuses: *"I'll get there eventually,"* we tell ourselves. But that's the voice of comfort, not progress.

The truth is, there's always a way to go faster if you're willing to look for it. Derek could have taken four years. He didn't.

But this wasn't about rushing or cutting corners—it was about moving with clarity and intention. He saw the standard pace for what it was: a choice, not a rule.

Most people accept the system's default speed because it feels comfortable. But comfort is a trap. It's sloth disguised as safety, inertia posing as progress. To go faster, you don't need to rush past everything; you need to focus on mastering the essentials and cutting away what doesn't matter. It's not speed *versus* depth—it's speed *through* depth.

The real question isn't, *Can you go faster?* It's, *What's holding you back?* The system wasn't designed for people who want more. If you know where you're going, there's no limit to how fast you can get there—so long as you're willing to push, adapt, and keep going when it gets hard.

It doesn't matter where you are in your career, there's one thing everyone should obsess over: the compounding rate of your learning. The earlier you start, the more time you give your knowledge to grow and multiply. In the fall of 2014, Sam Altman, president of Y Combinator, gave aspiring entrepreneurs advice that applies to anyone pursuing growth. He told them to strip away the distractions and focus on the essentials: "At YC, we tell founders to work on their product, talk to users, exercise, eat, and sleep—and very little else."

This principle applies across the board. If you don't have a product to work on, view yourself as the product. Every book you read, every conversation you have, every project you complete—it's all part of increasing your compounding rate of learning. As the late investor Charlie Munger famously quipped, "I constantly see people rise in life, who are not the smartest, sometimes not even the most diligent, but they are learning machines. They go to bed every night a little wiser than they were when they got up and boy does that help, particularly when you have a long run ahead of you."

Most people wait for breakthroughs. Learning machines don't. They seek out lessons, apply them, and iterate. That's what Walton, Bryant, Gretzky, and Sivers did. They weren't content to let experience trickle in passively. They hunted it down, extracted its value, and moved forward.

That's what ignoring the speed limit is about. Not moving recklessly, but realizing that it's a suggestion, not a rule. If you want to succeed in your Permissionless journey, get comfortable setting your own pace.

The faster you stop letting artificial speed limits hold you back, the faster you get to where you were truly meant to go.

6

EMBRACE OBSESSION

The best way to do great work is to find something you're obsessed with and work on it all the time.
— Paul Graham (Co-founder of Y Combinator)

BEFORE QUENTIN TARANTINO became a director who would win Oscars and reshape cinema, he spent five years working at Video Archives, a video rental store in Manhattan Beach, California. To most, it was just a job—a way to pay the bills and pass the time. But for Tarantino, it was something entirely different. He didn't merely rent out tapes or make casual movie recommendations; he immersed himself in cinema. Every work shift was an opportunity to learn, and every film was a lesson.

Tarantino devoured movies, watching some repeatedly until he could predict every cut and line of dialogue. He memorized scripts, cataloged directing techniques, and studied interviews with filmmakers. When Video Archives eventually closed in 1995, Tarantino bought the inventory and rebuilt the store in his own home. "I don't know anyone who knows as much about movies as Quentin," people who worked with him often said. His encyclopedic knowledge of film was no accident—it was the result of years of deliberate practice.

Even his own work, Tarantino admitted, was built on this foundation. *Pulp Fiction*, widely regarded as a cinematic masterpiece, was a mashup of stories and techniques borrowed from countless films he had studied. "The idea with *Pulp Fiction*," Tarantino explained, "was to take three of the oldest stories in the book." There's the hoodlum who has to take out the boss's wife but can't touch her. The boxer who's supposed to throw the fight but doesn't. The hitman who delivers cold justice.

"We've seen those stories a million times," Tarantino said. "I just thought: what happens if we put them together? What happens if we hang out with the bad guys all day long, instead of cutting away to the hero?" His years of obsessive study allowed him to innovate within the familiar, turning old tropes into something fresh and unforgettable.

Obsession often gets a bad rap. We're told to find balance, fit in, and not take things too seriously. But the truth is, obsession is a superpower. It's the force that propels you to go deeper than anyone else, to master your craft, and to create something extraordinary.

Take Jimmy Donaldson, better known as MrBeast. When Jimmy started uploading videos to YouTube, he wasn't an overnight success. His early videos—mostly gaming commentaries—struggled to find an audience. But Jimmy wasn't just making videos; he was studying the platform. He dissected analytics, tested titles and thumbnails, and analyzed audience behavior.

"There's a five-year stretch where basically every day I was just hyper-obsessed with YouTube. I watched every YouTube guide, read every article, studied every creator," Jimmy said in an interview.

This wasn't casual curiosity; it was obsession. By his late teens, Jimmy's fixation on YouTube had taken over his life. He'd spend hours testing video formats, optimizing retention, and brainstorming new concepts. His friends thought he was crazy. His mom gave him an ultimatum: go to college or move out. Jimmy chose the latter.

Today, MrBeast is one of the most successful creators in the world. His videos—ranging from elaborate challenges to philanthropic stunts—amass hundreds of millions of views. But his obsession hasn't wavered. He still pores over analytics, tweaking every detail to improve performance. "If you want to be the best at something, you have to be obsessed," he said. "You have to wake up thinking about it and go to bed thinking about it. You have to breathe it."

Obsession isn't about working hard for the sake of it. It's about finding the thing you can't *not* do—the thing that consumes your thoughts and fuels your energy. Here are a few ways to uncover your obsession:

1. The Pee Test: Pay attention to what you get so absorbed in that you forget to take care of basic needs (like peeing). The next time you lose track of time, ask yourself: What was I doing? Why did it pull me in so deeply?

2. The Midnight Test: What keeps you awake at night—not out of stress, but out of excitement? What would you willingly sacrifice sleep for, even if no one else noticed or cared?

3. The Boredom Test: What do you find fascinating that others find boring? Often, the activities you enjoy but others avoid hold clues to your unique strengths and interests.

Obsession has a way of clarifying priorities. It strips away distractions, forcing you to focus on what truly matters. It pushes you to go deeper, to learn more, and to work harder—even when the rewards are distant or uncertain.

Especially in the age of the internet, obsession isn't just an asset—it's a requirement for extreme success. Investor Naval Ravikant articulated this perfectly: "If you're not 100 percent into it, somebody else who is 100 percent into it will outperform you. And they won't just outperform you by a little bit—they'll outperform you by a lot."

The internet has changed everything. It has democratized opportunity. Anyone with an iPhone and a Wi-Fi connection can start a media company or launch a brand. That's the magic of the modern age. But it's also the challenge. If it's easy for you, it's easy for everyone else. The playing field is crowded, and the signal-to-noise ratio has never been lower. The only way to stand out is through an obsessive commitment to excellence.

EMBRACE OBSESSION

Obsession isn't something to fear; it's something to embrace. When harnessed correctly, it becomes the engine that drives action. It pushes you to go further, work harder, and think deeper than anyone else.

Ask yourself: *What are you willing to obsess over? What's the thing you can't stop thinking about, even if no one else understands it?*

Because when you find it, you won't need anyone's permission to chase it. You'll already be too far ahead.

7

BE A SUPER CONNECTOR

You can have everything in life you want, if you will just help other people get what they want.
— Zig Ziglar (Author and Motivational Speaker)

THE CANDLELIGHT FLICKERED across the wooden table. Ten men leaned in, debating the week's most pressing questions. The room smelled of ink and parchment, the air thick with ideas.

At the center sat Benjamin Franklin, 21 years old, a printer by trade. He had no wealth, no political power, no family connections to lift him up. But he had something just as valuable: a room full of sharp minds, each pushing the others forward.

Franklin called it the Junto, a gathering of ambitious men committed to improving themselves and their city. Each week, they met at a Philadelphia bookshop to discuss business, philosophy, and civic ideas. But this wasn't just talk. They tackled real problems. The Junto established America's first lending library, developed the city's first volunteer fire department, and planted the seeds for the University of Pennsylvania.

Centuries later, another young innovator applied the same strategy to remarkable effect.

At 19, Jimmy Donaldson, who we mentioned in the previous chapter, formed a mastermind group with fellow aspiring YouTubers. At the time, each member had around 10,000 subscribers—small in the world of online content. But what set them apart was their shared obsession with cracking YouTube's algorithm.

For 1,000 days straight, they met every single day to analyze what worked, what didn't, and how they could improve. They swapped feedback, dissected viral videos, and pushed each other to think bigger. Every member of the group eventually surpassed a million subscribers, a milestone that had once felt impossible. Today, MrBeast is one of the biggest creators on the planet, with a following in the hundreds of millions.

Franklin and MrBeast operated in different eras, but they understood the same principle: growth isn't a solo pursuit. The right group doesn't just add value—it multiplies it.

If you want to accelerate your career, expand your influence, or build something meaningful, the key isn't just working harder. It's surrounding yourself with people who challenge you, sharpen your thinking, and open doors you never knew existed.

Here's how.

Pro Tips for Becoming a Super Connector

1. Whenever you like something, tell the creator

Most people admire from a distance. They assume their praise won't matter, so they stay silent. But creators, founders, and industry leaders remember the people who take the time to say something—especially when that praise is specific.

- If an article shifts your perspective, email the author.
- If a podcast episode resonates, leave a thoughtful comment.
- If a book changes how you think, post about it and tag the author.

In a world where most people consume and move on, these small gestures stand out. Do this consistently, and over time, you'll go from a stranger to someone they recognize.

2. Don't be afraid to ask for help

Benjamin Franklin had a political rival who disliked him. Instead of trying to win him over with favors, Franklin asked to borrow a rare book from his library.

The rival, flattered by the request, lent him the book. Franklin returned it a week later with a thank-you note. From that moment on, the man became one of Franklin's biggest advocates.

This is the *Ben Franklin Effect*—when you ask someone for a favor, they subconsciously start to like you more.

Most people hesitate to ask for help, assuming it's a burden. In reality, people enjoy sharing their expertise—as long as it's the right kind of ask.

- **Keep it specific and thoughtful.** A vague *"Can I pick your brain?"* feels like work. A precise *"I saw you just crossed $100k/mo with your agency. Congrats! What was the script you used to land your first client?"* is much easier to answer.
- **Make it easy to say yes**. Keep it short. Show you've done your homework. If it's an intro request, write a quick blurb they can copy-paste.
- **Don't over-ask**. If someone helps you, take their advice, apply it, and follow up. No one wants to help someone who keeps asking but never acts.

You'd be surprised how often people say yes.

3. Be the initiator

Most people wait for someone else to create opportunities. They sit back, hoping to be invited. Super connectors build the spaces where relationships happen.

- Learning a new skill? Find others who want to learn it with you.
- Reading a book? Start a book club.
- Traveling to a new city? Host a dinner.

And it doesn't have to be a huge gesture. There's a concept I stumbled across called "Pebbling":

When male penguins want to show affection, they search for the perfect pebble. Not just any rock—a specific one. Then, they waddle over and offer it to their mate as a gift. If it's accepted, it becomes the first stone in the nest they'll build together.

I've always loved that image. Because it reminds me that every great relationship starts with a gesture. A signal. A small act that says, I see you. I care.

In practice, it's often something simple:

- You read an article and think, *This reminds me of that founder I met last week.* So you send it to them.
- You hear a podcast and text it to a friend going through something similar.
- You finish a book and immediately recommend it to someone you know would love it.

Those are pebbles. They take less than a minute, but they massively increase the trust and connection people feel with you.

At its core, being a super connector isn't about collecting contacts—it's about fostering ecosystems where ideas flourish and people grow.

Whether you like it or not, every opportunity comes from a relationship. Careers are built, deals are made, and ideas spread because someone put the right pieces together.

So ask yourself: Who are you bringing to the table?

8

LEARN TO SELL

A flower is a weed with an advertising budget.
— Rory Sutherland (vice chairman of the Ogilvy & Mather group of companies)

IN 1948, David Ogilvy walked the streets of a small Scottish village, knocking on doors with a near-impossible task. He was selling AGA stoves, a product most homeowners neither wanted nor cared about. At first, he focused on features and technical details. "This stove has even heat distribution," he'd explain with precision, but his words fell flat. Homeowners nodded politely, then closed their doors.

Exhausted and frustrated, Ogilvy stood on another doorstep, ready to deliver the same tired pitch. But something caught his attention—a faint aroma of tea wafting from inside. Watching the homeowner pour a steaming cup, he had an epiphany. She wasn't buying a stove. She was buying warmth, comfort, and the rituals of home.

This time, he set the pamphlet aside and spoke differently. "Imagine your family gathered around this stove on a cold evening. A hearty meal simmering, the room filled with warmth and the smell of home cooking." The homeowner's eyes lit up with interest. She bought the stove, and Ogilvy left with a new understanding of what it means to sell.

By the end of the year, Ogilvy was AGA's top salesman. He didn't succeed by mastering technical specifications. He succeeded because he understood human behavior. People don't buy products. They buy emotions, aspirations, and transformations.

Years later, Ogilvy carried this insight into advertising. His campaigns didn't just promote features—they told stories. The Rolls-Royce ad, famously stating that "the loudest noise in this new Rolls-Royce comes from the electric clock," didn't just sell a car. It sold luxury, precision, and status.

Before making any pitch, sale, or advertisement, Ogilvy first asked himself: *What does this person want?* Selling begins with understanding. If you want to connect with someone, ask questions first. Whether you're pitching an idea, negotiating a salary, or proposing a partnership, start by understanding the other person's perspective. What do they value? What problem are they trying to solve?

While Ogilvy learned to sell and became one of the most influential figures in advertising, not everyone masters this skill. Nikola Tesla, one of history's greatest minds, created ideas that could have reshaped civilization. Yet his inability to connect his vision with others left many of his innovations unrealized.

Tesla's brilliance was unmatched, but he struggled to frame his ideas in ways others could grasp. His proposals were often too abstract, too far ahead of their time, or simply unrelatable. Investors, like J.P. Morgan, became frustrated with Tesla's vague promises and grandiose visions.

Wardenclyffe Tower, Tesla's vision for wireless electricity, was shut down. The Death Ray, his invention to end all wars, never left the drawing board. His World Wireless System, an early version of global communication, was written off as science fiction. Tesla's failure wasn't due to a lack of brilliance. It was his inability to bridge the gap between his vision and the understanding of others.

Selling is not about manipulation or pressure. It's about connection. It's about understanding what people value and presenting your ideas in ways that resonate deeply. People decide with their hearts and justify with their heads. If you want to move others, speak to their emotions first, then back it up with logic. Ogilvy succeeded because he empathized with his audience and crafted messages that appealed to their emotions. Tesla's story, in contrast, serves as a reminder of what can be lost when that connection is missing.

Think about every opportunity you want. A job offer, an investment, a partnership—they all depend on your ability to make others believe in you. Even the best ideas, if left unsold, remain just that: ideas.

As author Sir Ken Robinson once said, "An idea is not worth much until it is shared. It is the sharing of ideas that propels society forward." Selling is not just a tool for business. It is essential for bringing your vision to life, no matter the field.

If you believe in your vision, you have a responsibility to make others believe in it too. This doesn't mean pandering or being inauthentic. It means listening, understanding your audience, and framing your ideas in ways that inspire action.

Ogilvy's lesson is clear. Mastering the art of selling is not optional. Ogilvy knocked on doors and made his ideas impossible to ignore. Tesla, for all his genius, struggled to do the same. The difference between them wasn't intelligence. It was the ability to make others see the value of what they created.

Learn to sell. It's the bridge between where you are and where you want to go.

9

DO THE WORK UPFRONT

A young man once asked Mozart how to write a symphony.
Mozart replied, "You're too young to write a symphony."
Frustrated, the man shot back, "But you were writing symphonies when you were 10, and I am 21!"
Mozart smiled and said, "but I didn't run around asking people how to do it."

IN 2017, Gerald Xavier wasn't a professional copywriter. He wasn't a seasoned marketer, a published author, or someone with a polished portfolio. What Gerald had was a keen eye for opportunity—and the guts to act on it.

Gerald first discovered *Impact Theory*, a business and mindset-focused interview show created by Tom Bilyeu, co-founder of Quest Nutrition. Drawn to Tom's mission of empowering individuals to break free from limiting beliefs, Gerald quickly became a devoted listener. But he wasn't content to simply watch from the sidelines. He spotted a gap that others overlooked—a missing piece in the *Impact Theory* ecosystem.

Despite its growing popularity, Tom's team wasn't sending a weekly newsletter. No updates on new episodes, no curated insights for fans, nothing. To Gerald, this wasn't just a missed detail—it was a golden opportunity.

He could have sent a message pointing out the gap. Maybe suggested the idea. But Gerald understood something most people don't: *value isn't in ideas—it's in execution.* So, instead of pitching, he went to work.

Over the next few days, Gerald immersed himself in *Impact Theory*. He dissected episodes, took notes on Tom's philosophy, and reverse-engineered how the brand communicated. Then, he wrote five sample newsletters, each one designed to look like it was already part of the brand's voice.

But even the best pitch is useless if it doesn't get seen. While Tom's Instagram and Facebook pages were overflowing with activity, his Twitter had far less traffic. Gerald sent a DM with the audacious opening:

If this isn't the best newsletter you've ever read, I'll donate $500 to the charity of your choice.

Attached was a link to the five newsletters he had written.

Within a week, Tom's team replied. For six months, Gerald wrote *Impact Theory*'s newsletter—for free. A year later, when the company decided to hire a full-time copywriter, Gerald was the obvious choice.

Gerald's story is about more than just boldness; it's about preparation. It's easy to look at what he did and think, *Wow, that was risky,* but it wasn't. Gerald didn't just wing it—he did the work upfront.

Most people don't. They'll send a vague DM, drop a half-baked pitch, or expect others to connect the dots for them. Then they're surprised when they're ignored. But the truth is, no one owes you a shot. If you want the attention of people who are already operating at a high level, you have to make it impossible for them to ignore you.

That's what Gerald did, and it's what you can do too. But it starts with research—the kind most people aren't willing to do.

If you want to work for someone you admire, partner with your dream company, or pitch a game-changing idea, here's how to do the work upfront:

1. **Dive into past conversations.**
   Search for podcast appearances, interviews, or articles featuring your target person or company. Pay attention to moments where their energy spikes or their curiosity shines. Look for gaps in the conversation—places where the interviewer moved on too quickly. These are your opportunities to add value.
2. **Use Twitter (X) like a pro.**
   Twitter is a goldmine for raw, unfiltered thoughts–especially from entrepreneurs. Use advanced search tools like Twemex or search parameters like "from:@handle min_faves:100" to surface their most significant tweets.

You'll gain insight into their priorities, challenges, and even their sense of humor.

3. **Go beyond the first page of Google.**
Most people never scroll past the first page of search results. But the juiciest insights come where most don't care to look. Use creative searches like "[name] + college" or "[name] + early career" to uncover hidden connections. These details can give you unique angles for your pitch.

4. **Explore the archives.**
Platforms like YouTube have filters that let you watch someone's oldest videos first. Their early work often reveals their original vision, unpolished experiments, or forgotten priorities. These insights can provide a fresh perspective others won't think of.

5. **Leverage your network.**
Sometimes, the best way to stand out is through a personal connection. Reach out to someone in their orbit—a former colleague, a friend, or even a past collaborator. Ask thoughtful questions like, "What's something they're passionate about that doesn't come up often?"

When you do this kind of work, you're sending a clear message: *I respect your time enough to come prepared.* It's not about asking for an opportunity—it's about showing you're ready for one.

Whether you're applying for a role, pitching a collaboration, or trying to break into a new industry, remember: the work doesn't start when you send the email or make the call. It starts long before that.

II

PART II: CREATION

WHAT IS CREATION? Creation is the act of turning potential into reality. It's about taking bold action, creating opportunities, and refusing to wait for permission. Creation demands courage and relentless effort. It's rarely neat or predictable—often messy, challenging, and full of surprises. In this section, we explore the art of stepping out of preparation and into the arena, embracing uncertainty, and bringing your vision to life.

10

STRIKE WHILE THE IRON IS HOT

"Someday" is a disease that will take your dreams to the grave with you. If it's important to you and you want to do it "eventually", just do it and course correct along the way.
   – Tim Ferriss (Author of The 4 Hour Workweek)

IN 1994, Jeff Bezos was at the pinnacle of a promising career.

As a senior vice president at a prestigious Wall Street firm, he was managing millions of dollars, surrounded by brilliant colleagues, and well on his way to long-term success. By all conventional measures, Bezos had already won the game.

But one statistic stopped him cold: internet usage was growing at an astonishing rate of 2,300% per year. Bezos couldn't get it out of his head.

Bezos lived by numbers, data, and probabilities. But this wasn't a calculation—it was a question of who he could become.

He took a long walk in Central Park with his boss, a man he respected immensely. Bezos laid out his idea for starting an online bookstore. It was ambitious and untested. Bezos's boss listened carefully before responding.

"That actually sounds like a great idea," his boss said. Then he paused. "But it sounds like a better idea for someone who doesn't already have a good job."

That line hit Bezos like a freight train. His boss wasn't wrong. Why would anyone leave certainty for chaos?

Bezos went home and wrestled with the decision. How could he know if this was the right move? How could he justify walking away from the life he had built?

That's when Bezos created what he called the *Regret Minimization Framework.* He imagined himself at 80 years old, reflecting on his life. Would he regret trying and failing at this idea? Or would he regret not having tried at all?

The answer came instantly: *He would regret not trying.*

"When you are in the thick of things, you can get confused by small stuff," Bezos later said. "But when you project yourself to age 80, you can clearly see the big decisions that matter."

So, Bezos packed up his life, left his prestigious job, and moved to Seattle. He started building his company out of a garage, with desks made of cheap wooden doors and a website that barely worked. Friends questioned his sanity. Coworkers dismissed his idea as impractical. The odds were against him.

But Bezos wasn't betting on guarantees. He was betting on potential.

Today, we know how the story ends: Amazon is one of the world's largest companies, and Bezos credits his decision to act in the face of uncertainty as the key to its success. He didn't wait for the perfect time—he created it.

Jeff Bezos wasn't the only one who recognized the fleeting nature of opportunity. Around the same time, a young man named Elon Musk stood at his own crossroads.

It was the summer of 1995. Musk had been accepted into a prestigious PhD program at Stanford to study material science. For most people, this was the pinnacle—a chance to secure a stable, respectable life in academia. But something gnawed at Musk.

The internet revolution is happening *right now*. He could feel it.

"It only happens once," Musk's boss, Peter Nicholson, told him. "The internet revolution only comes once in a lifetime, so strike while the iron is hot."

That advice hit home. Musk thought about his future: If he stayed in academia, the internet's greatest opportunities might pass him by. If he deferred Stanford and took a chance, he might fail—but he might also build something extraordinary.

So Musk deferred his PhD enrollment. Instead of attending Stanford, he co-founded Zip2, a startup that provided business directories and maps online. Musk worked around the clock, living in his tiny office and showering at a nearby YMCA. At night, when exhaustion set in, doubt would creep in too: *What if this doesn't work? What if I've made the wrong choice?* But in those quiet moments, he reminded himself of the alternative—staying safe, watching from the sidelines, and missing the revolution entirely. The odds weren't great. Most startups failed, and online businesses were seen as risky, but Musk decided that failing was better than not showing up at all.

Four years later, Compaq acquired Zip2 for $307 million. Musk's decision to seize the opportunity didn't just change his life—it set the stage for everything that came next: PayPal, Tesla, SpaceX.

Musk didn't need a perfect plan or permission to act. He understood what so many people miss: the opportunity was there—he just had to show up. "If something is important enough, you do it even if the odds are not in your favor," Musk later said.

Most people don't miss opportunities because they're not capable—they miss them because they're afraid. They settle for something safer, something easier—a life that feels deceptively comfortable but ultimately hollow. Steven Pressfield calls this a *shadow career*. It's the safer, watered-down version of the thing you actually want to do.

Pressfield writes, *"Sometimes, when we're terrified of embracing our true calling, we'll pursue a shadow calling instead. That shadow career is a metaphor for our real career. Its shape is similar, its contours feel tantalizingly the same. But a shadow career entails no real risk. If we fail at a shadow career, the consequences are meaningless to us."*

How many people have dreams of starting a business but stick to a corporate job they don't love because it's comfortable? How many would-be musicians dream of filling arenas but keep their songs in the shadows? How many aspiring artists sketch ideas but never share their work?

Both Bezos and Musk understood a truth most people ignore: *there is no perfect time to act.* Opportunities don't wait. They come, and they go, whether you're ready or not.

Bezos reframed hesitation as regret: *Will you look back and wish you'd taken the chance?* Musk saw it as urgency: *The revolution is happening now—don't miss it.* Neither waited for the perfect moment because they knew it didn't exist. Instead, they acted, despite not having any guarantees of success.

The challenge is clear: Will you take the leap, or will hesitation keep you on the sidelines? In the following chapters, you'll discover how people bet on themselves, acted before they felt ready, and turned small decisions into life-changing opportunities.

Strike while the iron is hot.

11

GO WHERE THE ACTION IS

If you want to catch a wave, you have to be in the ocean.
— Unknown

AT JUST FOURTEEN YEARS OLD, Taylor Swift stood in her family's kitchen, clutching a guitar case and looking up at her parents. Taylor grew up studying the careers of renowned country music artists Faith Hill and Shania Twain, noticing they all started in Nashville. That's where I need to be, she told her parents.

For years, Taylor had been writing songs in her bedroom, performing at local fairs, and dreaming of becoming a country music star. But no matter how many songs she wrote or how many shows she played, her small Pennsylvania hometown wasn't where country music happened.

Taylor had been persistent in her requests for years, repeatedly telling her parents, "If Faith Hill went to Nashville, then I have to go to Nashville." She knew that Pennsylvania wasn't going to open the same doors.

At fourteen, Taylor didn't just have ambition—she had clarity. She understood something most adults struggle with: talent alone isn't enough. You have to go where the opportunities are. For Taylor, that place was Nashville, Tennessee—the beating heart of the country music industry. Nashville was where the record labels, songwriters, and producers were. It was where the action was.

So, with her family's support, Taylor packed up her life into a moving van and headed south.

When they arrived, Nashville felt big, overwhelming. "It was like stepping into a dream," Taylor said years later. The city buzzed with music. Signs for live performances covered café windows, and the air seemed to hum with songs waiting to be written. But opportunity wasn't going to knock on her door. If Taylor wanted to make it, she had to go find it.

She and her mom drove up and down Music Row—a stretch of Nashville filled with recording studios and industry offices. Taylor, wearing a determined smile, walked into every building that would let her in. She carried a stack of demo CDs she'd recorded and handed them to anyone who would take one—receptionists, managers, producers.

Most people barely looked up. A few smiled politely, promising to pass the CD along. But Taylor noticed the piles of demo CDs already stacked on desks. She knew the odds were slim.

"It felt like no one was listening," she later admitted. "But I kept telling myself: someone will."

When the meetings went nowhere, Taylor focused on what she could control: performing. She played in cafés and fairs. She performed at songwriter nights and in parking lots, often to tiny audiences. She knew if just one person heard her, then it would be worth it.

And eventually, someone *did* hear her.

While performing at a café, Taylor caught the attention of a local music executive. He didn't just hear her voice—he saw her drive, her clarity of purpose, and her ability to connect with a room. Soon after, Taylor signed a deal with Sony/ATV Music Publishing, becoming the youngest songwriter in their history at just fifteen years old.

From there, things moved quickly. Taylor didn't just get a seat at the table—she proved she belonged there. She wrote tirelessly, refined her sound, and poured herself into her music. Not long after, she signed her first record deal and released her debut single. Her career took off, redefining country music and setting her on a trajectory that would make her one of the most iconic artists of her generation.

Taylor's story makes one thing clear: You can be the most talented person in the world, but if no one knows you exist, it doesn't matter. You have to put yourself in the right place and fight for it.

100 x 0 = 0

Skills   **Visibility**   **Opportunities**

Taylor Swift didn't wait for Nashville to come to her. She went to Nashville. And once she got there, she knocked on doors, played every stage she could find, and made herself visible. Her talent didn't change when she moved—her opportunities did.

The truth is, opportunity isn't evenly distributed. Certain places, industries, and communities act as amplifiers. They concentrate talent, energy, and resources in ways that make success more possible. Think of:

- **Silicon Valley** for tech innovators.

- **New York City** for finance and fashion.
- **Los Angeles** for entertainment.
- **Venice Beach** for bodybuilding.

Proximity doesn't guarantee success. But it increases your chances of it. It puts you in the room with the right people, exposes you to opportunities you wouldn't otherwise see, and forces you to level up.

You can't live big in a small environment. Stay in the wrong place too long, and you start to shrink. You talk like the people around you. You think like them. You want what they want. If no one around you is building something big, taking risks, or pushing for more, neither will you. Not because you aren't capable, but because you won't even realize you should.

But the second you step into a bigger room, everything changes. You see how small you were thinking. You feel what real ambition looks like. You stop making excuses and start making moves. If you feel stuck, look around. The problem isn't always you—it's where you're standing.

Now you might be thinking, *"What if I can't pack up and move to a city like Nashville or Silicon Valley."* Well, you're in luck. In today's digital world, proximity isn't always about geography. With social media, you can position yourself in the right rooms without leaving home.

- **Join Online Communities**: Find forums, Slack groups, or Discord channels where people in your field share ideas.
- **Attend Virtual Events**: Conferences, webinars, and live

Q&As bring the action to you.
- **Engage on Social Platforms**: Follow leaders in your space. Contribute to conversations. Make yourself known.

Opportunity doesn't come to those who wait. It comes to those who seek it out, position themselves where it matters, and refuse to be ignored.

Go where the action is. Then make your move.

12

MAKE YOUR MOVE

It had long since come to my attention that people of accomplishment rarely sat back and let things happen to them. They went out and happened to things.
— Leonardo Da Vinci (Italian Polymath)

IN 1971, Errol Gerson was just another MBA graduate in a sea of hopeful job seekers. Years later, he would become a celebrated business professor, teaching over 6,000 students in his lifetime. But back then, he was just a young professional, weighed down by a pile of rejection letters and an increasingly urgent question: *Why wasn't anyone calling him back?*

Determined to crack the code, Errol decided to do something different. He asked to see the résumés of his peers—the very people he was competing against for jobs. What he discovered was shocking: they all looked the same. Same font, same format, same lifeless presentation. His own résumé blended right in. It was competent but invisible.

Errol realized that if he wanted to break through, he couldn't rely on being "just as good as everyone else." He needed to stand out.

So, he experimented. He printed his résumé on thick, high-quality paper and made it slightly taller than a standard page by 1/8th of an inch. Then he swapped the usual Times New Roman font for Helvetica, giving his résumé a clean, modern look. These changes may sound trivial, but they had an outsized impact. When recruiters picked up the stack of résumés, Errol's stuck out—literally. Within days, he had a job offer.

Errol's story isn't about using fancy fonts or thicker paper. It's about making intentional moves that grab attention. He didn't have better grades or more connections than his peers. What set him apart was his willingness to think differently. That's what this chapter is about: making your move in a way that ensures you're seen, heard, and remembered.

Target the Right People

One of the biggest mistakes people make when trying to break through is aiming too high. Everyone wants to email Elon Musk or DM Beyoncé, thinking that if they could just get one reply, their lives would change. But here's the truth: people like Musk and Beyoncé aren't going to respond. It's not because they're rude—it's because they're already surrounded by people whose full-time job is to filter out requests like yours.

Even if you somehow get through, there's another problem: they likely can't help you. People at their level are too far removed from the challenges you're facing. It's the curse of knowledge. Musk doesn't remember what it's like to be an early-stage founder struggling to make rent. Beyoncé isn't thinking about how to book her first gig. Their advice, while inspiring, is often impractical for someone just starting out.

Instead, focus on people who are a few steps ahead of you. These are the individuals who've recently been where you are. They understand your challenges and can offer advice that's specific, actionable, and relevant. They're also far more likely to reply because they're not buried under a mountain of requests.

Think of it like climbing a ladder. Instead of trying to jump to the top, focus on grabbing the next rung.

Find the Open Space

Stephen Curry isn't just one of the greatest basketball players of all time—he's also a master of movement. On average, Steph runs 2.53 miles per game. His ability to find open space, move without the ball, and position himself strategically is what makes him so dangerous on the court. As Curry says, "If you're constantly moving, you're a threat."

The same principle applies to outreach. If you want someone to notice you, don't go where the competition is fiercest. Instead, find the cracks in their attention.

Let's say your target is a prominent author. Their email inbox is likely overflowing with requests, but their Instagram DMs might be quieter. Or maybe they're active on LinkedIn but only receive a handful of thoughtful comments on their Twitter/X posts. Those are the open spaces where you can stand out.

Outreach isn't about being loud. It's about being smart. By positioning yourself where your target's attention isn't overwhelmed, you increase your chances of being seen and heard.

Pro Tip: Everyone's trying to get the attention of "the guy," but almost no one thinks to reach out to "the guy's guy"—the producer, assistant coach, chief of staff, first hire, or research assistant. Those are the people who can actually make things happen.

Craft a Hook That Demands Attention

Most emails fail before they're even opened. Why? Because the opening line is generic and forgettable. Your first sentence needs to grab attention and spark curiosity.

Here are a few examples of strong hooks:

- "I've made an irreversible decision."
- "Your LinkedIn."
- "Big fan."

The key is to make your opening specific, personal, and intriguing. Don't try to impress them with buzzwords or flattery. Instead, be concise and make them want to open your email.

The rest of your message doesn't matter if they don't open the email.

A Cold Email Template That Works

Here's a simple, effective structure for crafting a cold email:

Subject Line: Make it personal or intriguing.

Example: "Quick idea for [Company Name]" or "Loved your post about [Topic]."

Opening Line: Start with why you're reaching out.

Example: "I've been following your work on [specific topic] and wanted to share an idea I think could help."

Body (2-3 sentences): Explain why you're worth their time. Highlight your research, skills, or past results.

Example: "I noticed [specific opportunity/challenge], and I'd love to help you [specific solution]. For example, I recently [relevant achievement or result]."

The Ask (1 sentence): Give first. Then be clear about what you want.

Example: "I recorded a 3-minute Loom video [about your solution]. If you're open to it, I'd love 15 minutes of your time to discuss this further."

Close: End with gratitude and your why.

Example: "Thanks so much, and I really admire [specific thing about them]."

Sample Email:

Subject: Quick idea for [Company Name]

Hi [Name],

I've been following your work on [topic] and wanted to share an idea I think could help. I noticed that [specific challenge or opportunity], and I'd love to help you solve it. For example, I recently [relevant achievement].

I recorded a 3-minute Loom video [about your solution]. If you're open to it, I'd love 15 minutes of your time to discuss this further.

Thanks so much, and I really admire [specific thing about them].

Best,
 [Your Name]

[LinkedIn or Website Link]

Follow Up Without Being Annoying

If you don't get a reply, don't take it personally. People are busy. A polite follow-up can often make the difference. The key is to follow up with value.

Sample Follow-Up Email:

Subject: Following up on my idea for [Company Name]

Hi [Name],

Just wanted to check in on my previous email. I'd still love to help with [specific opportunity]. In case you missed it, attached is a brief 3-minute Loom video detailing [specific challenge they have]. Let me know if there's a good time to chat!

Best,
   [Your Name]

Pro Tip: Use The Public DM: Most people send cold emails or DMs. That's level 1. Level 2? Reach out in public. Write a short post on Twitter (X) explaining who you are, what you admire, and how you can help. Tag the person—and then ask your friends to tag them too. It's simple: public messages get seen more. And when others vouch for you, it adds pressure to respond.

> **Pinned**
> **Jeston Lu** ✓ @jestonlu · Apr 8
> Feeling ambitious, going to shoot my shot:
>
> Hey @businessbarista, I'd love to work for you and your company @storyarb.
>
> Here's my pitch to help you with content strategy: 📌
>
> 💬 16   🔁 10   ❤️ 119   📊 42K

Here's an example of a "Public DM" from Jeston Lu, a sophomore in college:

> **Andrew Yeung** ✓ @andruyeung · Apr 8
> @businessbarista - @jestonlu is talented and worth chatting with!
>
> 💬 1   🔁   ❤️ 7   📊 764

Tons of people tagged Alex Lieberman in the comments and vouched for Jeston.

Errol Gerson didn't know for sure that his taller résumé would work. He didn't have a guarantee. But he took the shot. He made his move.

The same is true for you. Whether you're emailing a potential mentor, pitching a new idea, or applying for your dream job, the only way to make progress is to act.

Because the harsh truth is, if you don't ask, the answer is always no. So position yourself strategically, craft your message thoughtfully, then… make your move.

13

A SHAMELESS ASK

Speaking of making an ask... if you've made it to this part of the book, I'm going to take a wild guess: you didn't hate it. In fact, maybe you even liked it a little?

Modern books live and die by one thing—Amazon reviews. So, if this book made you pause, think, or (hopefully) take action, I'd be thrilled if you could leave a review.

Not only does it help more people find the book, but it also helps me win a bet with an author friend of mine that I can get more reviews than she does. No pressure... but I'd really like to win ;)

It only takes a minute, and I'd be eternally grateful. Here's how:

- **If you're on Audible** → Tap the three dots next to the title and select "Leave a review."
- **If you're on Kindle or an e-reader** → Scroll to the end, and you should see an option to leave a rating.

- **If neither of those work** → Just head to the book's page on Amazon (or wherever you bought it) and leave a review there.

Your support means the world—thank you for reading!

-Jay

14

CREATE YOUR OWN ROLE

The minute you understand that you can poke life, and something will pop out the other side—that you can change it, mold it—that's maybe the most important thing.

– Steve Jobs (Co-founder of Apple)

CREATE YOUR OWN ROLE

BY THE LATE 1990s, Tony Fadell was out of moves. He had joined General Magic straight out of college, drawn in by a team trying to build the future. They were working on ideas no one else could see yet—pocket-sized computers, digital assistants, connected devices. But the timing was off and the company folded.

He went to Philips next. It looked good on paper. Big brand. Big title. But nothing he worked on ever shipped. The culture was slow and he wanted more.

So he quit.

He launched a startup called Fuse. The goal was to build a new kind of modular device, one you could snap together like building blocks. It made sense to him. It didn't to anyone else. Investors pulled out. The money ran out.

And just like that, it was over. Fadell had no team, no company, no direction. Just a pile of burned-out ideas and a question he couldn't shake: *what now?*

"I was at rock bottom," Fadell would later say. Everything he had worked for seemed to have fallen apart.

Most people, faced with failure after failure, would interpret it as a sign. They might retreat to safer ground, scaling back their ambitions in favor of a stable, conventional career. But Fadell didn't see it that way. Instead, he looked outward and saw a world full of problems. One problem, in particular, caught his attention.

At the time, digital music was a mess. MP3 players were clunky, ugly, and frustrating to use. Their software barely worked, and organizing music felt more like a chore than a joy. People loved music, but no company had figured out how to make the experience seamless.

For most, the issue wasn't worth addressing. The technology seemed too limited, and the market appeared too niche. But Fadell saw it differently. "Why is no one solving this?" he wondered. The gap was glaringly obvious to him, and he couldn't let it go.

So he started building.

In a small room, armed with little more than a laptop, Fadell began obsessively prototyping. The idea wasn't just to create a better MP3 player—it was to design an entire ecosystem. The device, the software, the experience—every aspect had to work in harmony, transforming how people discovered, organized, and enjoyed their music.

The work was grueling, and the obstacles were endless. He pitched his concept to multiple companies, only to be met with rejection after rejection.

"It's too risky," they told him.
"It's a niche market."
"People don't want this."

But Fadell couldn't let the idea go. Despite the setbacks, despite the doubt creeping in, he kept refining, kept iterating. Finally, he secured a meeting with Apple.

Apple, at the time, wasn't the powerhouse we know today. The company had been struggling for years, its future far from certain. But Steve Jobs had returned, and with him, a vision to rebuild Apple into something extraordinary.

When Fadell pitched his idea for a new kind of MP3 player, Jobs saw potential. But he didn't immediately offer Fadell a high-ranking position or a team of engineers. Instead, he brought him on as a contractor—a precarious, uncertain role with no salary, no safety net, and no guarantees. It was a test. Could Fadell deliver?

"I wasn't being hired to follow orders," Fadell would later reflect. "I was there to create something that didn't exist."

Fadell threw himself into the work. The challenges were daunting. The batteries were too weak. The interface was clunky. Manufacturing costs were prohibitively high. Each problem felt insurmountable, yet Fadell and his small team tackled them one by one. They sourced better parts, streamlined the hardware, and refined the software until it felt effortless. Fadell obsessed over every detail, from the size of the scroll wheel to the intuitive simplicity of the user interface.

When the first iPod was unveiled in 2001, it was a revelation. Sleek, intuitive, and beautifully designed, it didn't just work—it felt magical.

"A thousand songs in your pocket," Jobs announced. The world had never seen anything like it.

The iPod didn't just change music; it changed Apple. It turned a struggling company into a cultural icon, laying the groundwork for the iPhone and the modern digital age.

Fadell's role at Apple grew alongside the iPod's success. He went from a contractor with no guarantees to Senior Vice President, overseeing the development of not just the iPod but also the iPhone. His vision for seamless, integrated technology helped Apple become one of the most valuable companies in the world.

Fadell didn't wait for someone to hand him an opportunity. He didn't wait for the perfect conditions or for the market to catch up. He saw a problem, pursued a solution, and executed.

Here's the uncomfortable truth: the roles we think we're waiting for often don't exist. They're not written up in job descriptions or handed out by managers. They're created by the people bold enough to see a problem and decide they're the one to solve it. Waiting for permission—or worse, waiting for someone else to solve it—only guarantees that nothing will happen.

But how do you take that first step? This is where the TAG Method from Charlie Hoehn comes into play. Charlie himself used this strategy to become director of special projects and right hand man to best-selling author Tim Ferriss.

Target. The first step is to pick a worthwhile target. Choose a company or individual whose work excites you, whose values resonate with yours, and whose success you want to amplify. Fadell's obsession with solving digital music wasn't random; it aligned with his deep love for technology and his desire to create seamless experiences.

Audit. Next, audit their work. Spend hours—if not days—diving deep into what they're doing, where their strengths lie, and where they're falling short. Understand their goals, their challenges, and the gaps they're not addressing. This is where you uncover opportunities to add value.

If you're preparing for an interview, think of it as solving a problem. Before you walk into that room, ask yourself: What's one challenge this company is facing, and how can I help solve it? Then, come armed with a solution—whether it's a concrete proposal, fresh ideas, or a small project you've created on your own. When you walk in prepared, you don't just show you want the job—you show them you're already thinking like part of the team.

Tony Fadell didn't wait for Apple to articulate their problems; he anticipated them. He didn't pitch a better MP3 player—he pitched a solution to the broader issue of how people discovered, organized, and enjoyed music. By the time he walked into that meeting, he didn't need to sell himself—his work did it for him.

Gift. Finally, offer them a gift. Show them how you can solve a problem they didn't know they had or help them achieve a goal they've been struggling with. Don't just tell them you're the right person—prove it by doing the work in advance. Create a prototype, draft a proposal, or map out a strategy. The key is to demonstrate your value before you're asked.

Pro Tip: So much of getting what you want is answering the question: "How can I make this a no-brainer for the other person?"

Jobs aren't given to the most qualified. They're given to the ones who make themselves impossible to ignore. If you want to stand out, stop applying blindly and start being deliberate. Pick a target. Study their problems. Show up with something valuable.

The world doesn't hand you permission to make an impact. The roles you want to play, the changes you want to see, the work you want to do—it's all waiting for you to create it.

> **Permissionless Challenge:**
> Use the TAG Method! Pick a target. Do an audit of their work. Send them a free gift. Don't expect to get anything in return. The act of doing the audit and reaching out is your prize. Everything else is upside.

15

DIVE THROUGH CRACKED DOORS

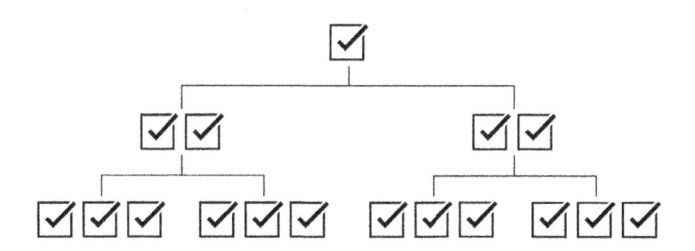

Opportunities multiply as they are seized.
— Sun Tzu (Chinese Military Strategist)

BY THE TIME SIDNEY WEINBERG RETIRED, he had

transformed Goldman Sachs into one of the most respected financial firms in the world. But Sidney didn't come from privilege. He didn't attend an Ivy League school, inherit connections, or start with an impressive job title. In 1907, at the age of 16, he took a job as a janitor's assistant at Goldman Sachs, earning just three dollars a week. To anyone else, it looked like the bottom—a dead-end job with no future.

But Sidney didn't see what everyone else saw. He saw something more: opportunity.

On his first day sweeping floors at Goldman Sachs, Sidney Weinberg was struck not by the scale of the work but by the scale of the world around him. The firm's partners strode confidently across marble floors, barking orders and discussing deals that Sidney didn't yet understand. He noticed the stacks of papers, the constant movement of messengers, and the buzz of deals being made all around him. He was surrounded by power, influence, and wealth—and he was a teenager with a broom.

Most would have been discouraged by the gulf between where they were and where they wanted to be. Sidney wasn't.

When he wasn't sweeping, he observed. When he wasn't observing, he helped. He ran errands for the firm's partners, organized mail, and memorized everything he could about how the firm operated. He was quiet but deliberate, always looking for ways to be useful.

One day, while delivering mail, Sidney overheard a senior

partner searching for someone to help organize stacks of client paperwork—a small task, but one no one had volunteered for.

"I'll do it," Sidney piped up, the words leaving his mouth before he had fully thought them through.

The partner glanced at him skeptically. "You sure, kid?"

"I'm sure," Sidney replied firmly.

The task was tedious. Sidney spent days sorting through piles of files, reorganizing them in a way that made sense. When he handed the finished work back, the partner was impressed. "You're a sharp kid," he said. "Let me know if you want to help with something else."

That moment—one cracked door—changed Sidney's trajectory. For the first time, he felt noticed. He had proven himself reliable, resourceful, and capable of handling more than a broom.

Over time, Sidney's willingness to take on small, thankless tasks gave him access to more and more opportunities. When no one else wanted to do a job, Sidney raised his hand. He wasn't thinking about the prestige or the payoff—he was thinking about how much he could learn.

He moved from sweeping floors to running errands. From running errands to working in the mailroom. Every job brought him closer to the decision-makers at Goldman Sachs. And every day, he absorbed more about how the business worked—how deals were made, how clients were managed, and how fortunes were built.

By the time he was 30, Sidney had risen to the level of partner—a feat almost unthinkable for a former janitor's assistant.

But Sidney's story wasn't just about hard work. It was about how he approached every opportunity, no matter how small. He saw grunt work not as beneath him but as a stepping stone. He knew proximity to the firm's leaders was invaluable, and every task he took brought him closer to the people who could change his life.

Sidney's story is a reminder of what happens when you set ego aside and focus on proving your worth through action. Most people let their pride get in the way. They look at the small tasks and think, *That's not my job. I'm better than this.*

The truth? Those tasks—the ones that look insignificant, thankless, or beneath you—are often the cracked doors to something far greater.

Contrast Sidney's story with that of countless employees who refuse to help on projects outside their job description. They save themselves time in the short term but lose valuable exposure, trust, and momentum in the long term.

Sidney wasn't concerned with titles or credit. He was concerned with progress. He understood that small opportunities—even the ones that look insignificant or unglamorous—are often where the real leverage lies.

DIVE THROUGH CRACKED DOORS

In 1933, during the depths of the Great Depression, Goldman Sachs faced immense challenges. Businesses were failing, markets were collapsing, and the firm needed someone they could trust to secure new opportunities.

Sidney Weinberg was that person. After years of proving himself reliable, capable, and sharp, he was now in a position to lead. That year, he secured one of Goldman Sachs' first major government contracts during the New Deal. It was a turning point for the firm, and it solidified Sidney's role as its leader.

He went on to serve as CEO, steering Goldman Sachs through decades of growth and cementing its reputation as one of the most respected firms on Wall Street. Sidney built his legacy not on privilege or luck but on his ability to spot cracked doors and dive through them.

Opportunities rarely come gift-wrapped. They don't announce themselves with fanfare or arrive on a silver platter. More often, they look like grunt work, thankless tasks, or minor roles in the background.

The people who succeed aren't the ones who wait for perfect circumstances—they're the ones who act. They seize what's in front of them and prove their worth through action.

Sidney didn't stumble into success. He created it. By saying yes to small opportunities, he positioned himself for bigger ones. By acting like he already belonged, he earned his seat at the table.

16

GIVE THE EXTRA OUNCE

At 211 degrees, water is hot. At 212 degrees, it boils. And with boiling water, comes steam. And with steam, you can power a train.
— Sam Parker (Author of 212: The Extra Degree)

WEST VIRGINIA'S MEN'S BASKETBALL COACH Bob Huggins wasn't exactly excited to be watching an 8 a.m. AAU game.

The basketball court was tucked into the farthest corner of the tournament's sprawling complex, surrounded by a dozen other games playing simultaneously. Huggins, a two-time National Coach of the Year, had seen thousands of high school players by that point in his career. Most early-morning games were uninspired—the kind where players jogged through warmups and loafed through fast breaks.

Huggins sipped his coffee, trying to shake off the morning haze, when something caught his attention.

There was a kid—Jevon Carter—pressuring the ball full court, tirelessly, while everyone else barely broke a sweat.

"He was picking up full court, pressuring people from end line to end line," Huggins recalled. "But no one else on his team was pressing. Just him."

Most players treat early games as a warmup. Coaches don't expect much effort. They're just looking for flashes of skill. But here was Carter, turning an otherwise mundane game into a personal showcase of intensity and grit.

Huggins called his assistants. "We've got to sign this guy," he said.

"What does he do well?" they asked.

"Hell, I don't know what he does well," Huggins said. "But he sure tries to guard."

It wasn't just that Carter was giving effort. It was *how much* he gave, and *when*. At 8 a.m., with no scouts demanding it, Carter did the extra thing—the thing that separated him from a thousand other players Huggins had watched.

Carter's effort earned him a scholarship to West Virginia, where he became the face of the team's signature defense, earning the nickname "Press Virginia." His work ethic was legendary. He showed up early, stayed late, and outworked everyone in the gym. That same relentless approach carried him to the NBA, where he became a defensive specialist–hounding the league's top scorers, forcing turnovers, and doing the gritty, unglamorous work that often goes unnoticed on the stat sheet. Coaches loved him because they knew one thing for sure— Carter would outwork anyone on the court, every single night.

Jevon Carter's story reminds me of a parable I once heard.

There once was a father with three sons, all of whom worked at the same fur trading company. The first son earned $100 a week, the second $300, and the third $500. Curious about the pay gap, the father asked the company president why.

The president decided to show him.

He called in the first son and said, "There's a ship at the dock called *The Ontario*. I hear it's carrying furs. Check it out and report back." The son made a call and returned in five minutes. "They have 1,500 seal furs," he said.

The president thanked him and called in the second son. He gave the same instructions. An hour later, the son came back and said, "I went to the dock. They have 1,500 seal furs in excellent condition."

Finally, the president called in the third son. The same instructions. Four hours later, the third son walked into the office and said, "I went to the dock. They have 1,500 seal furs, all in top condition, so I bought them at $5 each. I also found a buyer willing to pay $7, so I sold them. While I was there, I noticed they had 39 mink furs, which I know you like to handle personally. I've put a hold on them for an hour so you can inspect them. Is there anything else I can do?"

The president turned to the father and said, "That's why."

The first son did the bare minimum. The second did what was asked. But the third son? He gave the extra ounce.

What separates those who stand out isn't just their talent or even their skill—it's how much further they're willing to go. Jevon Carter could have coasted like everyone else at 8 a.m., but he didn't. The third brother could have made the same call as his siblings, but he didn't. They stood out by doing more, by being unmistakable in their contribution.

But what does this look like for you?

If you're an artist, it might mean doing an extra revision even when you think your piece is done. If you're an entrepreneur, it might mean doing your research and preparing a pitch deck for your sales meeting. If you're a recent graduate, it could be sending a handwritten thank-you note after an interview instead of just an email. Each extra ounce you give creates opportunities that wouldn't have existed otherwise.

Most people do what's expected. They clock in, finish their tasks, and go home. They play their part. But the people who truly succeed—the ones who rise above the noise—are the ones who ask, *What else can I do?* They don't stop at 'good enough'. They find ways to do more than their share.

The truth is, normal behavior is forgotten. Nobody tells stories of when you do the expected. They only tell stories when you go the extra mile. When you stay late to reformat a presentation that no one asked you to fix, but that ends up landing the client. When you show up to practice an hour early to practice, to get extra reps while your teammates are still stretching. When you remember your friend's favorite snack and bring it to the movie night just because you know it'll make them smile.

Doing what is expected costs nothing in the short term but fades into obscurity. Going above and beyond costs a little more—effort, time, energy—but it creates a ripple effect that lasts. The extra ounce may not always pay off immediately, but over time, it builds something invaluable: reputation capital.

The extra ounce isn't glamorous. It often means doing the unglamorous work—the things no one asks you to do but everyone notices when they're done. It's not always rewarded right away. But the people who consistently give more than what's asked find that the rewards come eventually, and they're worth the wait.

The question is simple: Will you stop at good enough, or will you push for just a little more? Will you do what's expected, or will you be the one who goes the extra inch, the extra rep, the extra hour?

In the end, will you be remembered for simply showing up—or for going above and beyond?

17

WORK IN PUBLIC

Work with your garage door up.

Writing books, recording podcasts, tweeting, and YouTubing–these kinds of things are permissionless. You don't need anyone's permission to do them.

– Naval Ravikant

WORK IN PUBLIC

IN THE SMALL CANADIAN TOWN of Stratford, Ontario, 13-year-old Justin Bieber sat cross-legged on the living room floor of his modest home. The camera was nothing special—a borrowed device, grainy and unsteady. His backdrop wasn't a professional studio or a well-lit stage; it was the couch his family gathered around after dinner. But as soon as he started singing, the room fell away. It was just him, the melody, and the hope that someone out there might be listening.

He uploaded that first video to YouTube without much fanfare. No one in Stratford knew what YouTube could do; in 2007, it wasn't yet a springboard for stardom. Bieber didn't have a plan. He only had a desire—to sing, to be heard, to share something with the world.

The video didn't go viral overnight. At first, a few friends watched it, then family members. Then strangers. One video turned into ten, then twenty. The videos weren't perfect. Oftentimes the lighting was bad, or the audio crackled. But what they lacked in production value, they made up for in authenticity.

Bieber wasn't polished, but he was real. And that was what people connected with.

Years later, Scooter Braun, a well-known music talent manager, couldn't remember exactly how he stumbled onto Bieber's channel. It might have been a random click or a video suggested by the algorithm. But he remembered the moment he saw Justin singing Ne-Yo's "So Sick." There was something undeniable about it. Braun was mesmerized. The boy's raw talent and natural charisma practically leapt off the screen.

"I couldn't stop watching," Braun would later say. "There was just this spark—this something that you can't teach, and you can't fake. I knew immediately that I had to find this kid."

Braun spent hours combing through Bieber's YouTube channel, watching every video. He wasn't just impressed by Justin's voice—though that alone set him apart. It was his consistency, his confidence, and his willingness to share himself, flaws and all. Here was a kid with no professional training, no studio setup, no team—and yet, he had managed to captivate an audience. Braun knew that kind of authenticity couldn't be manufactured.

How was this kid not already signed?

Braun tracked Bieber down, called his mother, and convinced them to fly to Atlanta to meet him. The moment Justin walked into the room, Braun knew he hadn't been wrong. He introduced Bieber to Usher, a Grammy-winning singer, who saw the same potential Braun had. What followed was a meteoric rise that defied every industry norm. Record deals. Sold-out tours. Global fame. But none of it would have happened if Bieber had waited to be "ready." Those grainy videos—the ones he probably wished were better—were what got him noticed.

This is the part of the story most people miss. Putting yourself out there isn't easy. It's terrifying. It's easier to keep your work hidden, to tell yourself, *I'll share it when it's ready. I'll wait until it's perfect.*

But while you're waiting, someone else is hitting publish. Someone else is taking the risk you won't. The truth is, you'll never feel fully ready. And your work will never be perfect. But the people who succeed are the ones who show up anyway. They don't let fear stop them. They understand that the work you hide doesn't help anyone—not you, and not the people it's meant for.

Sharing your work isn't just about visibility—it's about momentum. Each post, each upload, each release becomes a signal to the world: *I'm here. I'm working. I'm serious.* It invites feedback. It attracts collaborators. It plants seeds.

James Clear, author of *Atomic Habits*, calls this "manufacturing your own momentum." As he puts it, "You can attract luck simply by telling people what you are working on." The world can't help you if it doesn't know what you're doing.

Outbound vs. Inbound Personal Marketing

Most people only market themselves when they need something—a job, a promotion, an opportunity. But that's like waiting until you're starving to start looking for food.

The trick is to market for the job you want before you need it. Build a body of work that signals what you're about. If you do it well, the right opportunities will find you.

- **Outbound Personal Marketing** is cold emails, applying for jobs, pitching yourself to people who don't know you. It's better than doing nothing, but it's exhausting.
- **Inbound Personal Marketing** is making sure your name stays top of mind. When you work in public, opportunities come to you. You don't have to pitch yourself constantly—your work does it for you.

Selling Your "Sawdust"

One of the simplest ways to work in public is to document your process. Most people think they need a finished product before they can share anything. They don't. The journey itself is valuable.

When carpenters craft fine furniture, they leave sawdust on the floor. The best craftsmen find ways to repurpose every scrap. If you've already done the work, share the byproducts.

- If you're a musician, share behind-the-scenes clips of your recording process.
- If you're an athlete, show your training routine.
- If you're an entrepreneur, document the creation of your product.
- If you're building a skill, share what you're learning along the way.

People don't just want results. They want to see how things are made. By working in public, you build trust, visibility, and momentum—all before you "arrive."

In the internet age, working in public has never been easier. Social media platforms give creators direct access to an audience without the need for gatekeepers. Anyone can share their work, test ideas, and build momentum.

When you work in public, you invite critique. Yes, some feedback might sting. But often, it's the catalyst for improvement. The things you can't see in your own work are often obvious to others. A poorly lit video on YouTube can still teach you how to improve your lighting next time. A half-baked idea shared online can attract someone with the insight or skills to help you finish it.

Think of Justin's YouTube videos as seeds. He didn't know which would sprout. But by planting so many, he increased the odds that one would land in front of someone like Scooter Braun. And that's exactly what happened.

Justin Bieber's first videos weren't polished. They didn't need to be. They simply needed to exist. He didn't wait for the perfect camera or studio. He used what he had. What he created in those moments—flawed as they might have been—was enough to change his life.

Work in public. Sell your sawdust. Hit publish.

Permissionless Challenge:
Publish something today. Don't overthink it. Don't wait until it's perfect. Just ship.

- Share a behind-the-scenes look at what you're working on
- Post a short lesson you've learned this week
- Document your process: what you're building, writing, or struggling with

The goal isn't to go viral. The goal is to manufacture momentum.

18

GET IN THE ARENA

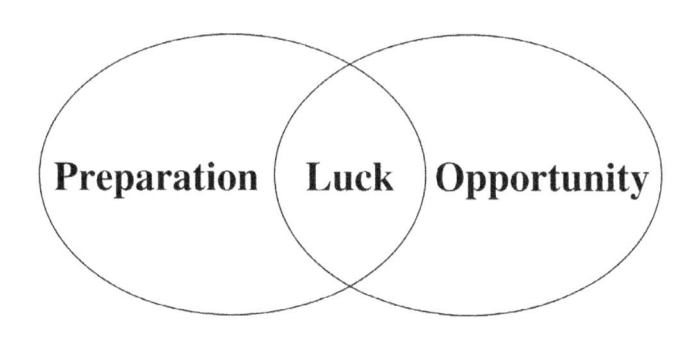

Preparation | **Luck** | **Opportunity**

Opportunity dances with those already on the dance floor.
— H. Jackson Brown Jr. (Author of Life's Little Instruction Book)

PREPARATION IS ESSENTIAL, but it's only half the battle.

Too many people spend their lives collecting tools they never use. They bury themselves in research, tweak plans endlessly, and constantly seek the "perfect advice", mistaking busywork for real progress. But the truth is simple: action, any action, is better than none.

Ask yourself: how long have you been waiting for the perfect moment? Waiting for everything to fall into place. Waiting until you feel certain, capable, or qualified. Waiting for some invisible signal to tell you it's time.

Most people never begin. They cling to the illusion that someday conditions will align perfectly. But the harsh truth is "someday" never arrives.

Instead, you have to get in the arena.

At age 19, Steven Spielberg had already been rejected by every major film school he applied to. By most measures, he had no reason to believe he would ever make it in Hollywood. But Spielberg wasn't the kind to sit back and accept someone else's definition of his potential. When traditional paths closed, he found his own.

He enrolled at a local community college in Los Angeles—not because he cared about the classes but because he knew proximity mattered. If he wanted to make films, he needed to be near the people making them.

One day, Spielberg found himself on a Universal Studios tram tour. While tourists snapped photos of soundstages and mock neighborhoods, he was watching something else—the people behind the scenes. Directors giving instructions. Technicians setting up equipment. Crew members working in synchronized chaos. It was a world he wanted to step into, not just observe from the sidelines.

As the tram slowed near a soundstage, Spielberg made his move. He slipped out of his seat, crouched low, and darted behind a building. The tram rumbled away, oblivious to the stowaway it left behind.

The air hummed with activity—distant voices echoing off walls, footsteps on concrete, the clatter of equipment. Spielberg wandered through the lot, pretending to belong. He walked past crew members with the confidence of someone who had every right to be there. His heart pounded, but he kept moving, soaking in everything around him.

It didn't take long for someone to notice.

"Hey! Who are you? What are you doing here?"

Spielberg froze. He turned to see a man staring at him, clipboard in hand, his expression a mix of suspicion and curiosity.

Spielberg could have lied. He could have run. But instead, he told the truth.

"I'm 19 years old," he said, his voice steady but earnest. "I've always wanted to be a director. I jumped off the tram because this is where I need to be."

The man raised an eyebrow, then smiled. His name was Chuck Silvers, the head of Universal's Television Library. Something about Spielberg's audacity, his unpolished sincerity, struck a chord. Instead of throwing him out, Silvers handed him a three-day visitor's pass.

"Come back tomorrow," he said.

Spielberg did. Each morning, he arrived early, wandered through sets, watched directors at work, and asked questions. He made the most of every minute until the pass expired.

Then he came back anyway.

On the fourth morning, Spielberg greeted the same security guard with a casual "Morning, Scotty!" and walked onto the lot like he belonged. The guard waved him through without a second thought. Spielberg spent the next few months turning Universal into his personal school, observing how films were made, one scene at a time.

Eventually, Silvers found him again. But this time, his message was different.

"You've got hustle, kid," Silvers said. "But stop schmoozing. Don't come back until you have something to show for it."

Spielberg took the advice to heart. For months, he disappeared, pouring his energy into a short film called *Amblin'*. When he returned to Universal, Silvers was impressed enough to pass the film to Sidney Sheinberg, the studio's vice president. Sheinberg was so taken with Spielberg's work that he offered him a contract on the spot, making him the youngest director to ever sign with a major studio.

Spielberg wasn't born a film genius. He got rejected by every major film school he applied to. But instead of waiting for an open invitation, he took his career into his own hands.

The lesson is clear: you don't need to wait for the stars to align. You don't need every question answered or every tool in your toolbox. What you need is the courage to act—even when the path isn't clear.

As Theodore Roosevelt famously said, "It is not the critic who counts; not the man who points out how the strong man stumbles, or where the doer of deeds could have done them better. The credit belongs to the man who is actually in the arena, whose face is marred by dust and sweat and blood…"

The arena isn't comfortable. It's messy and unpredictable. You will fail—probably often. But failure in the arena is infinitely better than regret on the sidelines.

So stop waiting. Stop hesitating. Take the leap. Jump off the tram. The world doesn't reward spectators—it rewards the ones who dare to step into the field, no matter how unprepared they feel.

19

STAY IN THE GAME

NO, NO, NO, NO, NO, NO, NO, NO
NO, NO, NO, NO, NO, NO, NO, NO
NO, NO, NO, NO, NO, NO, NO, NO
NO, NO, NO, NO, NO, NO, NO, NO
NO, NO, NO, NO, NO, NO, NO, **YES**

I have not failed. I've just found 10,000 ways that won't work.

– Thomas Edison (American Inventor)

JAMES DYSON WAS EXHAUSTED. Every day, he retreated to

a garage behind his English countryside home—a space with no heat, no water, and no electricity. His mission? Build a vacuum cleaner that didn't rely on dust bags.

It was 1979, and the idea seemed absurd. Vacuum cleaners had worked the same way for nearly a century. Major manufacturers scoffed at the concept. Dyson believed in the potential of a cyclone-based design, an idea inspired by industrial dust separators used in factories. But belief alone wasn't enough.

For five years, Dyson toiled alone, constructing prototype after prototype. By the end, he had built 5,127 versions of his machine. Most didn't work. Many outright failed. Each failure revealed a flaw to correct, each iteration brought him closer. And each day tested the limits of his resilience.

"I would crawl into the house every night covered in dust after a long day, exhausted and depressed," Dyson later admitted. "There were times when I thought it would never work, that I would just keep making cyclone after cyclone, never going forward, never going backward, until I died."

It wasn't just the physical toll. Dyson's relentless pursuit strained his finances, his relationships, and his spirit. At one point, he mortgaged his home to keep the project alive, a decision that placed immense pressure on his family. His wife, Deirdre, supported the family by teaching art and painting, ensuring they could make ends meet during these challenging times. Friends questioned his sanity. Investors turned him away. At times, he felt utterly alone. But he kept going, driven by a vision that wouldn't let him quit.

In 1993—14 years after he tore the bag off his Hoover Jr. and 5,127 prototypes later—Dyson launched his first vacuum cleaner: the DC01. Unlike anything else on the market, it quickly became a sensation. Within a decade, Dyson had disrupted a century-old industry and built a billion-dollar company.

But the real lesson isn't in the triumph, it's in the grind. Dyson didn't wait for perfect conditions. He didn't let failure stop him. He stayed in the game long enough to get lucky. He later remarked, "There is no such thing as a quantum leap. There is only dogged persistence – and in the end, you make it look like a quantum leap."

This idea—that persistence and iteration beat perfection—has been demonstrated in fields far beyond engineering. One Florida art professor, curious about the relationship between practice and mastery, designed a simple yet revealing experiment with his pottery students. On the first day of class, he divided them into two groups with very different assignments.

The first group was told they'd be graded on quantity. The more pots they produced, the higher their grade. The second group, however, was tasked with creating just one pot—but it had to be flawless.

By the end of the semester, the results were clear: the best pots—the ones with the most creativity, skill, and craftsmanship—came from the quantity group. While the "quality" group spent their time theorizing and chasing perfection, the "quantity" group got to work. They experimented, made mistakes, and refined their techniques through repetition. Each attempt taught them something new, sharpening their skills with every pot they created.

Quality beats quantity, but the path to quality is paved with quantity.

This truth applies to every craft. English singer-songwriter Ed Sheeran likens creativity to turning on a dirty faucet. "When you switch it on, it's going to flow shit water for a while," he says. "But if you keep it running, eventually clean water will flow." Great ideas don't emerge fully formed. They're the result of bad drafts, failed attempts, and messy first tries.

Still, there's a balance to persistence. Not every idea is worth pursuing indefinitely. Not every failure is a lesson worth enduring. The key is distinguishing between giving up and pivoting.

Giving up means abandoning your vision entirely, often due to the discomfort of failure or the length of the journey. Pivoting, however, means adjusting your approach while staying true to your core vision. It's about being flexible in your methods but steadfast in your goals.

When manufacturers refused to license Dyson's technology, he didn't abandon his dream. Instead, he pivoted to producing the vacuum himself.

Within 18 months, the DC01 became Britain's best-selling vacuum cleaner. And today, Dyson's technology is the standard for vacuum cleaners worldwide.

Reflecting on his journey, Dyson remarked, "The failures taught me more than the successes ever did. It's why I kept going."

James Dyson didn't invent the perfect vacuum cleaner on his first try—or even his hundredth. The Florida students didn't make great pottery by theorizing. Ed Sheeran didn't write chart-topping songs without first writing terrible ones. Perfection is the result of imperfection embraced.

So, if you're waiting for the perfect moment, the perfect plan, or the perfect first draft—stop.

Give yourself permission to be imperfect. Build your 5,127 prototypes. Turn on the dirty faucet. And then stay in the game long enough to get lucky. Because the only way to create something extraordinary is to embrace the ordinary mess along the way.

20

TRY THE HANDLE

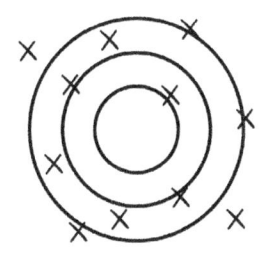

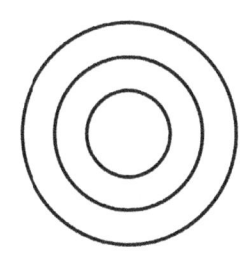

This Isn't Failure   **This Is**

The pessimist sees difficulty in every opportunity. The optimist sees opportunity in every difficulty.
— Winston Churchill (Former British Prime Minister)

IN THE 2016 film *Bleed for This*, there's a moment that stops you in your tracks. Vinny Pazienza, the boxer who defied all odds to step back into the ring after a near-fatal car accident, sits across from his trainer. The question comes like a jab, sharp and deliberate:

"What's the biggest lie you were ever told?"

Vinny doesn't hesitate. "It's not that simple," he says.

"Why not?"

"No, that's the biggest lie," he says. "That's how they get you to give up. They say it's not that simple, so you stop trying. But the truth? If you just do the thing they say you can't, then it's done. And you realize—it *is* that simple. It always was."

The room in the movie feels heavy with clarity, but the weight of that moment isn't fictional. It's a reminder of a truth most people ignore.

Life is full of locked doors. They appear everywhere—career paths you think are closed, opportunities you believe are out of reach, challenges you tell yourself are too complicated to tackle.

Most people walk past them without a second glance, convinced the handle won't turn. The artist who hesitates to show their work, believing they think it's not perfect. The entrepreneur who waits for funding before making a single move. The recent graduate who skips applying to their dream job, assuming they don't meet every qualification. The athlete who never sends their highlight tape to coaches, afraid of "bothering them".

But the truth is, most locked doors aren't locked at all. It's a mirage. We tell ourselves we don't have the resources, the talent, or the permission to try. But those are just stories we've been taught to believe. Where others see a dead end, you have to ask, "What if?"

Because when you train yourself to see opportunities, you realize they're everywhere. That job you thought required certain credentials? Someone with no degree just walked in and proved they could do it. That business you thought needed funding? Someone launched it with zero dollars and a Twitter account. That person you thought was out of your league? Someone with half your confidence went up and said hello.

Opportunities don't announce themselves. They don't come with neon signs or guarantees. They come disguised as challenges, hidden behind obstacles, and arrive wrapped in uncertainty.

Taylor Swift didn't wait for record labels to come to her; she moved to Nashville. Derek Sivers didn't wait for permission to start teaching himself music theory. Jony Ive didn't wait for a role at Apple to open up; he created his own role. None of the people in this book waited for an invitation. They stepped forward before the world knew their names, before anyone believed in them, before they were ready.

The harsh truth is this: The world is divided into two groups.

Those who wait—and those who don't.

You don't need perfect timing, the best credentials, or anyone's approval. You need the courage to step into the unknown, the willingness to fail, and the resilience to try again.

Sidney Weinberg didn't wait to be noticed at Goldman Sachs; he noticed where he could add value. MrBeast didn't wait for someone to show him how to succeed on YouTube; he experimented, obsessively, until he cracked the code. Steven Spielberg didn't wait for permission—he snuck onto a Universal Studios lot, made himself impossible to ignore, and landed a directing contract before he was 21.

Each of them made the same quiet decision: to begin, even when the path was uncertain. To create, even when failure seemed inevitable. To persist, even when others told them no.

The next time you're tempted to tell yourself, *It's not that simple,* stop. Ask yourself: What if it is? What if all that's standing between you and the thing you want is the courage to test the handle?

Because the truth is, you'll never know unless you try. And when you do, you might just find that the door wasn't locked after all.

If you take anything from this book, let it be this: the world isn't waiting to give you permission. The opportunities you want won't come from sitting still or following someone else's script. They come from taking bold, independent action—sharing your ideas, creating your own momentum, and stepping forward before you're ready.

That's the essence of *You Can Just Do Things*. You don't need a road map, just a direction. You don't need every answer, just the willingness to ask better questions. What you want isn't out of reach. The only question is: will you begin?

You don't have to wait. You never did.

Now, it's your turn.

Go make it happen.

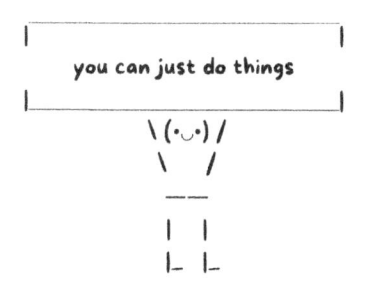

```
 _____
|                        |
|  you can just do things |
|_____|
         \ (•‿•) /
          \   /
           ——
          |  |
          L  L
```

PERMISSIONLESS REFLECTION

20 High Agency Questions to Ask Yourself:

1. **Don't Burn the Boats.** Am I building a strong enough foundation where I can capitalize on any future opportunity?
2. **Define Your North Star.** Do I know exactly what I want, and what I'm trying to avoid?
3. **Be a Learning Machine.** Where am I paying ignorance debt without even realizing it?
4. **Reverse Engineer the Greats.** Who has already solved the problem I'm facing, and what can I learn from them?
5. **There's No Speed Limit.** What am I treating as a rule that's really just a suggestion?
6. **Embrace Obsession.** What am I willing to go deeper than anyone else on?
7. **Be a Super Connector.** Who am I bringing to the table, and how am I helping them win too?
8. **Learn to Sell.** Do I have the skill set to make others believe in what I believe?
9. **Do the Work Upfront.** Have I done enough upfront preparation to show my commitment and competence?
10. **Strike While the Iron Is Hot.** If I don't act now, will my 80-year-old self regret it?

11. **Go Where the Action Is.** Am I spending time in rooms where opportunities actually happen?
12. **Make Your Move.** How can I deliver my pitch in a way that's impossible to ignore?
13. **A Shameless Ask.** What would I ask for if I wasn't afraid of hearing no?
14. **Create Your Own Role.** Where can I create my own role instead of waiting to be picked?
15. **Dive Through Cracked Doors.** What small opening can I wedge my foot into right now?
16. **Give the Extra Ounce.** What's the tiny bit of effort others aren't willing to give?
17. **Work in Public.** Am I sharing my work and processes in public, so others can notice and help?
18. **Get in the Arena.** Am I doing the real work, or just watching from the sidelines?
19. **Stay in the Game.** How can I be impatient with my actions and patient with the results?
20. **Try the Handle.** What bold move have I been too scared to try, and what would happen if I just tried the handle?

ACKNOWLEDGMENTS

SIR ISAAC NEWTON is quoted with saying, "If I have seen further, it is by standing on the shoulders of giants." This book would not exist without the giants—both past and present—who paved the way and lent me their shoulders to stand on.

To the incredible thinkers, writers, and creators who've shared their ideas with the world: thank you for being my teachers, even if we've never met. From midnight YouTube rabbit holes to dog-eared books and podcast binges that powered my early morning workouts, you've inspired me. Anything wise in this book came from their brilliance—I can only hope I've been a good steward of their ideas.

To my mom: thank you for showing me what hard work truly looks like—for leading with patience, kindness, and empathy in everything you do. Our long conversations, whether about business, life, or whatever topic we get lost in, are the highlight of my day. You've shaped not just how I think, but who I am.

To my dad: thank you for being my quiet force in the background, making sure I had everything I needed to pursue my ambitions. From setting up payments to navigating the legal and financial maze of starting a business, you handled the details so I could focus on building. Your support gave me

ACKNOWLEDGMENTS

the freedom to bet on myself. I couldn't have done this without you.

To both of you: more than anything, thank you for believing in me—always. No matter what project I tackled or what path I chose, your unwavering support (and patience) gave me the confidence to take risks and chase my ambitions. I'm beyond lucky to have you in my corner.

To Tyler Denk, EJ White, and the beehiiv team: thank you for taking a chance on an unproven high schooler. You gave me my first shot, and it changed everything.

To Noah Kagan: thank you for showing me what it means to build a dream life, and to have fun while doing it.

To Paul Millerd & Alex Wieckowski: thank you for your guidance on navigating the complexities of book writing and publishing.

To Jeremy Mary: thank you for being in my corner, championing my work, and sharing opportunities I didn't even know to look for.

To my ghostwriting clients, both named and unnamed: you've trusted me to tell your stories and bring your ideas to life. Those experiences have been invaluable, and I'm honored to have worked with each of you.

To the early readers of this manuscript: Noah Zender, Tim Forkin, Elijah Leopoldo, Max Yang, and others—thank you for your thoughtful feedback. Your insights made this book far better than it would have been otherwise.

To friends, family, and everyone who encouraged me along the way: your support has meant the world to me.

And if I've forgotten anyone, please forgive me. Feel free to add your name here:

_____.

Finally, to you, dear reader: life is short, and you chose to spend some of your precious time and attention with this book. I don't take that lightly. Thank you.

– Jay Yang (March 2025)

FURTHER READING

If you want more ideas, stories, and strategies for living and working permissionlessly, you can find me in a few places:

- **Join My Newsletter**: jayyanginspires.beehiiv.com
  Every week, I share insights on creativity, entrepreneurship, and personal growth, straight to your inbox.
- **Connect with Me**:
- Twitter (X): @jayyanginspires
- Instagram: @jayyanginspires
- LinkedIn: @jayyanginspires

I'd love to hear from you—what you liked, what resonated, or even how you've started taking action after reading this book. Drop me a message or connect with me on any of these platforms.

SELECTED BIBLIOGRAPHY

Author's note on stories:

The stories shared in this book are based on real events, drawn from biographies, interviews, documentaries, articles, and public records. In some cases, minor details have been dramatized or paraphrased to enhance clarity and narrative flow, but every effort has been made to preserve factual accuracy and represent events truthfully.

Where possible, sources have been cited directly or included in the Selected Bibliography. If you're curious about a particular story, I encourage you to dive deeper—many of the people featured here have remarkable books, speeches, and interviews that inspired this work.

This book is not a work of fiction. The people are real. The actions they took are real. The only question is: what action will you take?

Books

Arnold, Arnold Schwarzenegger. *Arnold: The Education of a Bodybuilder.* Simon & Schuster, 1977.

Cheney, Margaret. *Tesla: Man Out of Time.* Simon & Schuster, 2001.

Ellis, Charles D. *The Partnership: The Making of Goldman Sachs.* Penguin Books, 2009.

Fadell, Tony. *Build: An Unorthodox Guide to Making Things Worth Making.* Harper Business, 2022.

Gretzky, Wayne. *Gretzky: An Autobiography.* HarperCollins, 1990.

Hoehn, Charlie. *Recession-Proof Graduate: How to Land the Job You Want by Doing Free Work.* Self-published, 2013.

Isaacson, Walter. *Benjamin Franklin: An American Life.* Simon & Schuster, 2003.

Isaacson, Walter. *Elon Musk.* Simon & Schuster, 2023.

Jorgenson, Eric. *The Almanac of Naval Ravikant.* Self-published, 2020.

Kleon, Austin. *Steal Like an Artist: 10 Things Nobody Told You About Being Creative.* Workman Publishing, 2012.

Lazenby, Roland. *Showboat: The Life of Kobe Bryant.* Little, Brown and Company, 2016.

McBride, Joseph. *Steven Spielberg: A Biography.* University Press of Mississippi, 1999.

Nathan, Ian. Quentin Tarantino: The Iconic Filmmaker and His Work. White Lion Publishing, 2019.

Ogilvy, David. *Confessions of an Advertising Man.* Atheneum, 1963.

Parrish, Shane. *Clear Thinking: Turning Ordinary Moments into Extraordinary Outcomes.* HarperCollins, 2023.

Schroeder, Alice. *The Snowball: Warren Buffett and the Business of Life.* Bantam Books, 2008.

Thompson II, Marcus. *Golden: The Miraculous Rise of Steph Curry.* Atria Books, 2017.

Walton, Sam. *Sam Walton: Made in America.* Bantam Books, 1992.

Kagan, Noah: *Million Dollar Weekend.* Portfolio Penguin, 2024

Films & Documentaries
Bleed for This. Directed by Ben Younger, Open Road Films, 2016.
Miss Americana. Directed by Lana Wilson, Netflix, 2020.

Articles & Online Sources
Entertainment Weekly. "Taylor Swift's Road to Fame." *Entertainment Weekly*, 2008.
Music Business Worldwide. "Taylor Swift Re-Signs with Sony/ATV." *Music Business Worldwide*, https://www.musicbusinessworldwide.com/taylor-swift-re-signs-with-sony-atv/.
Fansided. "Jevon Carter and Bob Huggins' Story." *Fansided*, 2018, https://fansided.com/2018/03/16/jevon-carter-bob-huggins-west-virginia-recruit/.
Scotty Kessler. *Parable of the Three Sons.*, https://scottykessler.com/competition/3rd-son-story/.
Pressfield, Steven. *More from "Turning Pro." StevenPressfield.com*, https://stevenpressfield.com/2012/06/more-from-turning-pro/.

Videos & Podcasts
The School of Life. "Benjamin Franklin's Life Lessons." *YouTube*, uploaded by The School of Life, https://youtu.be/cLRLEnPaJLM?si=5mq_vB0sJEscFIo-.
Alex Hormozi. *How to Become a MILLIONAIRE This Year! (Shift Your MINDSET!) YouTube*, https://youtu.be/WK-d4H7xtvQ?si=t7e3a66-lQeA9TdG.
TEDxShanghaiSalon. *Power of the Mind. YouTube*, https://yo

utu.be/9_tYXFbgjZk?si=lilylJ9HAMRW0Ty3.

Scooter Braun. *On Being Enough, Insecurity, Wealth, Investing, Fame, Marriage and Much More.* YouTube, https://youtu.be/hx5KZPSgfuM?si=J_JIjkqVwqBMvesP.

Other References

Clear, James. Quote on X (formerly Twitter.), https://x.com/JamesClear/status/1263511239793217536.

Randolph, Marc. *Quote on X (formerly Twitter).*, https://x.com/mbrandolph/status/1713725065106530394.

About the Author

Jay Yang believes you don't need permission to create your own opportunities.

At 16, he cold-emailed Tyler Denk, CEO of beehiiv, with a list of ideas on how he could help. That email turned into an internship where he built *beehiiv 101*—a course that has helped hundreds of users unlock the platform's potential.

At 17, he sent Noah Kagan, founder of AppSumo, a 19-page pitch deck breaking down gaps in his social media and email marketing—and how to fix them. That landed him a role as Head of Content, where he led social media campaigns, including the one that made *Million Dollar Weekend* a *New York Times* bestseller.

Today, Jay continues to help entrepreneurs scale their brands, grow their audiences, and market their products more effectively.

When he's not working, he's likely playing pickup basketball, lifting weights, or spending time with family and friends.

You can connect with me on:
- https://jayyanginspires.beehiiv.com
- https://x.com/Jayyanginspires

Subscribe to my newsletter:
- https://jayyanginspires.beehiiv.com/subscribe

Printed in Great Britain
by Amazon